Divine Healing

God's Recipe for
Life and Health

by
Norvel Hayes

HARRISON HOUSE

Tulsa, Oklahoma

Unless otherwise indicated, all Scripture quotations are taken from the King James Version of the Bible.

Divine Healing: God's Recipe for Life and Health

ISBN: 978-168031-018-4

(Formerly *The Healing Handbook* ISBN 0-89274-704-8 and *How To Triumph Over Sickness* ISBN 0-89274-702-1)

Copyright © 1995 by Norvel Hayes
P. O. Box 1379
Cleveland, Tennessee 37311

Published by Harrison House Publishers
P. O. Box 35035
Tulsa, Oklahoma 74153

Contents

Introduction

People everywhere need to know about God's healing power, and they need to know the ways they can receive their healing.

In some churches people are taught how to pray for the sick, but most of the sick don't know how to receive their healing. It's terrible to be sick and not know how to get healed.

It's the simplest thing in the world for you to be healed: just obey the Scriptures and show God respect for His Word. It says, **He sent his word, and healed them** (Psalm 107:20).

Because the Lord has given me a healing ministry, He has dealt with me to share about the different phases of healing. There are different ways you can be healed, different things you can do. You need to learn in fine detail what to do by getting God's Word on the inside of you.

You can get God's Word inside you by sitting under good Bible teaching, but just going to church services won't heal you. The best church in the world isn't as good as the Gospel according to Matthew, Mark, Luke and John. You have to study the Bible for yourself. You have to look up chapter and verse. Then you have to quote it and claim it. You have to believe it and say, "That's mine—I've got it, in Jesus' name!"

When you learn from God's Word what you're supposed to do and that you're obligated to obey it, that Word will work for you every time. Healing works for everyone who obeys Him.

Once God's Word is inside you and you start quoting it, God will start performing it. **God looks over His Word to perform it** (Jeremiah 1:12). He wants you to have whatever you need, but you have to claim it. Unless you get the Word inside you, it'll never come out of you.

When you were born again by the Spirit of God, you became a citizen of heaven. As heaven's citizen, you've gained the right to anything heaven offers, just like any American citizen has the right to anything America offers. That means you have a right to healing. All you have to do is claim your rights.

As you read these pages about God's healing power, give the Holy Ghost your attention. When it's settled in your spirit once and for all that you can be healed, I guarantee it: You *will* be healed!

1

Your Faith Can Heal You!

The best way to receive healing is through your own faith.

Your beliefs are based on the way you were taught. Was everything you were taught really true? According to First Corinthians 12:2, **Ye know that ye were Gentiles, carried away unto these dumb idols, even as ye were led.**

The way you believe God today is the way you were led to believe. Think about where you are today. If you were taught according to the Scriptures, then you believe God according to the Scriptures.

If you listen to people who listen to God, who know Him and the Bible, you'll find it easier to believe the Bible and you'll be led according to the Scriptures. If your belief is based on the Word, God can easily manifest Himself to you through healing.

Base Your Beliefs on God's Word

Many people in churches today are ignorant of God's blessings because they've never really been taught about them. Some people think it's "weird" to believe in things like miracles, healing and casting out of devils. But it isn't weird—it's scriptural!

If you're sick and God heals you, it's not weird—it's a blessing based on the Bible. But you've got to find out what the Lord Jesus said and start obeying Him. Show God respect for

His Word, and He will heal you.

Now faith is the substance of things hoped for, the evidence of things not seen (Hebrews 11:1). Your faith is your substance and God's Word is your substance. Your faith needs to be based on God's Word.

> **But without faith it is impossible to please him: for he that cometh to God must believe that he is, and that he is a rewarder of them that diligently seek him.**
>
> **Hebrews 11:6**

First, you must have faith in what the Bible actually says. The Scriptures cover everything people need: salvation, miracles and healing.

Second, you have to diligently seek God by grabbing hold of the Scriptures. Be like a tiger that's crazy with hunger—just refuse to turn loose. Faith as the substance means showing God that you'll do something—right now!

Sickness Is Not From God

Maybe some kind of serious affliction has come on your body. Maybe you think you're dying. But I want you to realize that you don't have to die. Death is an enemy of God.

God doesn't put sickness or disease or any kind of affliction on the human race. No sickness or disease comes from heaven because none can be found there. God is the Boss of heaven, and He doesn't create disease so it can be put on human bodies to cause them heartaches.

The real enemy of God—the devil—is the cause of all sickness and disease. It's God's will to heal everybody, and it's God's will to heal *you*. God's Word is His will.

The Bible is God's perfect will for us to live by. But if we don't know what the Bible says, we can't live by it. Humans tend to live by suggestions that come to them through the power of the devil.

Satan will always try to tell you that you should rely on religion or your own way of doing what you want to do. Then he will be able keep your physical being from serving God. He tries hard to keep you away from a church that believes the Bible. A big trick he plays on human beings is to get them involved in any church that doesn't believe in healing.

Healing, as well as salvation, is a part of the Atonement, but Satan will try to get you to doubt it, overlook it, or just ignore it. Not only does he want to destroy you mentally and spiritually, but he wants you to doubt that God really cares anything about your physical well-being. If you have no faith in the healing power of the Lord Jesus Christ then you're giving the devil right of way, or free access, to attack your body.

The enemy wants to keep you from what the Bible actually teaches. You see, the Bible is the Truth. There's no other truth on the face of the earth for you or anybody else.

Knowing the Truth

In John 8:32 Jesus said, **And ye shall know the truth, and the truth shall make you free.** Jesus never tells a lie. That means everybody who knows the truth will be set free.

But it isn't just the truth that makes you free; it's *knowing* the truth that makes you free! You see, Jesus bore your sins, but He also took your infirmities and bore your sicknesses. (Isaiah 53:4, 5; 1 Peter 2:24) If you don't know that, you won't be made free. God's Word is the Truth!

The New Testament is the covenant you live under. The

word *testament* means covenant, an agreement between two or more parties. It's your responsibility to find out what the New Testament covers, because everything written in it is for your benefit. It's for you because God is no respecter of persons. (Acts 10:34) What Jesus did for others, He will do for you. Remember that!

God Wants To Heal *You*

Some churches teach the idea that God can heal you if He wants to. But that's far from what the Bible teaches. Jesus won't give sight to the blind person who just says, "If the Lord wants to heal me, He will." God can't work through that kind of believing.

God could heal people in every church in America and around the world if they knew that He could. But they won't be healed if they don't know that God will heal them.

God can only perform for you according to what you know. The part of the Bible you know as truth is what God will give you. If you haven't made up your mind that God will give you what the Bible says He will, then He won't.

Church leaders have to believe God's healing power is available to them. A church will be weak as long as weak men are in authority.

God works only through the strength in His Church. Jesus, the Head of the Church, gave all the power He had to the Church. (Luke 10:19) He isn't going to do anything else. As believers, we are His Church today. We've been given His name and His power. All power is in Jesus' name! (Matthew 28:18; Mark 16:17, 18)

All we have to do is obey Him. It's up to us to talk about God's healing power, to shout about it, sing about it and praise

God for it. That'll help bring it into manifestation. The sooner you realize that, the sooner you'll use His name to fight against the devil.

God's healing power will cause a cripple to come up out of his wheelchair and be made normal. It will heal a deformed child right before your eyes. But people in the average church don't know or believe that. Until they do, God's healing power won't come into manifestation in their church.

You have to prove it to people by reading the right Scripture verses to them. You have to hold up the Bible in front of your congregation and say to them, "God's healing power is available to you; all you have to do is learn how to get it."

If you don't tell people God's healing power is available to them, it'll never come to them. A deformed person could go to the same church every Sunday for fifty years, but if he never knows that God's healing power is available to him, he will never be healed.

If you are saying, "God will heal me if He wants to," you are letting doubt come in. God wants to do everything the Bible says He'll do, but He'll only do it for you if you believe it.

God's Test

Remember, God wants to heal *you*. No matter what might be wrong with you, God can hardly wait until you pass His test.

One time God explained to me what "passing His test" meant. He said: "The Bible is My test. My salvation verses are a test for sinners. My healing verses are a test for the sick. My miracle-working verses are a test for people who need a miracle. Son, when people look to Me as their miracle worker, I create things for them."

The Lord Jesus is personal; He becomes to you exactly what *you* say He is according to His Word. If you don't call Him *your* healer, He won't be. If you don't call Him *your* miracle worker, He won't be. He becomes to you exactly what you say He is. He'll fulfill all your needs. He'll heal you, make you strong, clear your mind, and give you peace.

I never have sad or confusing days. Now sometimes the devil will try to put confusion on me, but I won't accept it. There may be a few seconds of confusion, but I recognize it immediately and say, "No, I won't be confused. I take authority over you, Satan. In Jesus' name, go from me!" When Jesus gives me peace in my mind, confusion can't stay.

God wants you to keep His peace. It's hard to believe the Bible when you lose His peace. God doesn't answer prayers that are prayed from nervous faith, and He doesn't bless ignorance. If you're sick and stay ignorant of what God says about healing, He'll let you die. The test to be passed is over chapter and verse.

When you get born again and become God's child, you have a right to all the "goodies" found in Matthew, Mark, Luke, John, Acts, Romans and the rest of the Bible. That's your inheritance from God. He loves you individually, and He loves your body individually. He can hardly wait to heal you. Not only will He heal you when you believe Him for it, but He'll delight in doing it.

I went to grade school with a boy named Jimmy Maynor who was a midget. He just stopped growing at age 12, but he was completely normal otherwise. When he graduated from high school, he was four feet nine inches tall and weighed ninety-two pounds. He was called "Pee Wee."

Today Jimmy is six feet one inch tall! He passed God's test! Let me explain what happened.

While still a midget, Jimmy was riding in a car that was hit head-on by a drunk driver. The impact loosened Jimmy's leg bones and drove them through his hips until they were protruding out his back. Doctors in Cleveland, Tennessee, couldn't do anything for him, so he was sent to Chattanooga. Doctors there said he was like a bunch of hamburger meat, so they just put him in a room to die.

Jimmy had been unconscious since the wreck, but one night he woke up just long enough to cry out to God. He begged God to let him live. He said: "Lord, I don't want to meet You like this. You've tried to get me to work for You, but I wouldn't. I was rebellious. But, Jesus, if You'll heal me, I'll work for You as long as I live."

To the doctors' amazement, Jimmy woke up the next morning!

After about a week, two-pound weights were tied on Jimmy's feet to pull his leg bones back through his hips. In about a month, the bones were back in place.

Through the entire ordeal, Jimmy had been praying and reading the Bible. But then one day, a spirit of fear came into him when he overheard a conversation between the doctor and a nurse.

Thinking Jimmy was asleep, the doctor said, "It's a shame about what's happened to this little fellow. I don't know whether he'll live, but if he does, he'll never walk again. There's just no hope."

After staying in the hospital nine months, Jimmy's family took him home in an ambulance. One day as he was reading the Bible, he found out that the spirit of fear comes from the devil!

For God hath not given us the spirit of fear; but of

power, and of love, and of a sound mind.

2 Timothy 1:7

When he read that, he said, "Spirit of fear, I break your power over my life. I will walk again and be normal!"

Slowly, his body began to grow. Ten months and several pairs of trousers later, at the age of twenty-six, Jimmy was six feet one inch tall!

He then began to share his testimony in churches, telling people about what God had done for him. He drew large crowds, and the people were amazed when they heard his story.

One night Jimmy asked me to go with him to a meeting. When we got together, he said, "Norvel, I've had constant pain ever since that car wreck years ago."

He was surprised to hear my answer. I said: "Jimmy, you don't have to put up with pain; I don't. You need to get baptized in the Holy Ghost and receive power from on high to take authority over that pain. Don't take anything from the devil."

He got excited about that. Soon afterward, he asked God to baptize him in the Holy Ghost, and the Spirit of God came upon him.

Jimmy learned how to take authority over pain. When he found out what God had for him, he passed God's test, and he used his own faith to receive his total healing.

Don't Be Ignorant of God's Healing Power

Denominational churches don't know very much about God's healing power; but in some of them the people aren't ashamed of salvation. Their members are bold about John 3:16, and their ministers preach some of the best sermons in the world. But what you learn from those salvation sermons won't help when the devil comes against you with some physical affliction.

People in the church where I was raised didn't know anything about having healing services. Members of my church would say, "God can heal if He wants to; God can do anything." But that's a cop-out.

As long as you're ashamed of the Gospel, God will never heal you. If you're ignorant of what the Word says about healing, the devil can come in and claim your life.

The people in my church who took diseases died. There was no such thing as a blind person receiving sight or even a bad cold getting healed.

But God's Word says, **With his stripes we are healed** (Isaiah 53:5). To believe God, you have to pray and read the Bible. You have to work at it. When you believe God *can* do anything, He *will*.

2

Your Body Is a Living Sacrifice

God loves you. His healing power is a gift. All you have to do is receive it as a gift. Your sick body can be healed by faith in God's Word. God wants your body to glorify His name.

In the past, has your body been working for God? If not, and a disease has come into your body, you need to follow some advice from the apostle Paul. In Romans, chapter 12, he says:

> I beseech you therefore, brethren, by the mercies of God, that ye *present your bodies a living sacrifice, holy, acceptable unto God,* which is your reasonable service.
>
> And be not conformed to [or patterned after] this world: but be ye transformed [or completely changed] by the renewing of your mind, that ye may prove what is that good, and acceptable, and perfect, will of God.
>
> **Romans 12:1, 2**

It's Up To You

Realize right now—and never forget—that it's up to you what you do with your body; it's not up to anybody else. You're a free, moral agent. Either you will follow God's instructions and present your body to God, or nothing will ever be done about it. You alone will reap the consequences.

Paul wasn't writing this letter to people of the world—in

other words, sinners. He was writing to saints, the Christians in Rome: **To all that be in Rome, beloved of God, called to be saints ...** (Romans 1:7).

God wants you to have a well, strong, healthy body. Jesus wants you to live an abundant life, enjoying all the benefits provided for you in the New Testament. He wants every part of your body to walk in Him and function normally. If there's any affliction in your body, it was put there by God's enemy,—the devil.

Your faith can heal you, but your faith has to be founded in God's Word. His Word applies to all the beloved of God, those who are called to be saints. As Paul said, **I beseech you therefore, brethren...that ye present your bodies.** *You* have to do something with your body. *You* have to present it (or bring it) to God. If *you* don't do anything with it, nothing will ever be done with it.

In our churches, people have cluttered up some teaching until their minds are all confused. It's real hard to get the truth over to them because of what they've been taught in the past. The truth is, it's only what the Bible says that counts. And as we saw before, the Bible says, **He sent his word, and healed them** (Psalm 107:20). You can't know the truth until you really read and study God's Word. You have to take what He says at face value.

People who are against the Bible are always trying to explain it away. They want to destroy the idea of accepting it as truth. But you have to be honest with God and with yourself. You have to know the truth and believe the truth without questioning it, then that truth will make you free! (John 8:32)

In Romans 12:1, Paul didn't say to present only your inward self to God, the way some people interpret this verse. Paul said,

Present your bodies a living sacrifice. Present your physical body to God. We are to present our physical bodies to God for healing, for strength, for power and for health so that we can better serve Christ.

People in religious circles have missed this point. They just want folks to join their churches and do better. But salvation is more than just joining a church and doing better; it's a new birth!

I never have just tried to live right. Since I was born again, I've been living right because I became a new creature inside. **Therefore if any man be in Christ, he is a new creature: old things are passed away; behold, all things are become new** (2 Corinthians 5:17). When we're truly born again, our desires, appetites, ambitions and affections change. We're new creatures in Christ Jesus. The devil has tried to defeat me by temptations, by lying to me and trying to deceive me. When he would try to bring old habits and sin back into my life, I'd just fall down before the Lord, praying and asking Jesus for help. And His mighty power has never failed me!

Living a moral life is good, and I'm all for it. But living a moral life doesn't make you a Christian, and it won't take you to heaven. Being born again by God's Spirit is what takes you to heaven. Living a moral life is just religion, and religion isn't Christianity. Christianity is being Christlike, being born again and receiving God's gift of eternal life.

When eternal life—the nature and life of God—is put into your spirit, it changes you. It's easy then for you to read the Bible and it's easier for you to believe it.

But the devil doesn't give up so easily. He will keep reminding you of the things you've been taught in the past. He wants you to rely on what others have told you instead of what God's Word says.

Accept Jesus as Your Healer

You have to make up your mind to accept God's Word just as it is. God's Word is truth, and there's no other truth that can build your faith to the point where you can believe God. As you believe God's Word, your faith can heal you!

When you're born again by the Spirit of God, the inward man (your spirit) is changed, but the outward man (your body) doesn't change automatically.

The only thing that can change the condition of your body is for you to accept Jesus Christ as Healer. To do this, your faith has to be founded in the Scriptures that teach healing. As you release your faith, God's healing power will come into your body against the part that's afflicted by sickness or disease. His power will drive out that sickness if you stand steadfast by faith in God's Word and don't waver.

After the inward man becomes a new creature in Christ by the Spirit of God, he will have some trouble with the flesh; that is, fleshly temptations. People often say you have to die out to your old self, but that's wrong. When you've been born again, you don't have to die out to your old self; a new self has been put in place of the old. That new self is the nature of God, and the born-again child of God can begin to think like God thinks by renewing his mind to God's Word.

What you have to do after the new birth is die out to the flesh. Your flesh is the same body and flesh as it was before you were saved; but your new man, who is born from God, is a new man in Christ.

This new man inside you has to be fed the right kind of food, which is the Word of God. God's Word is the only kind of food available in this earth to feed your spirit and make you strong enough to believe God. **So then faith cometh by hearing, and hearing by the word of God** (Romans 10:17).

Don't Ask Your Body Anything

Your spirit won't get stronger than your body unless you read and study the Bible. God's Word is what feeds your spirit and gives it strength so that you can have faith not to listen to your body, or in other words, to the reasoning of your natural senses.

Don't give in to the dictates of your body (the fleshly self). Instead, feed the real you (the inward man) with the right kind of food—God's Word. You do this, and you'll find that your faith will get stronger and stronger.

Do as Paul did. He said, **I keep under my body, and bring it into subjection** (1 Corinthians 9:27). Paul meant that he kept his body under the subjection of his spirit. You can't do that unless your spirit is strong, so you need to daily feed it with God's Word.

Remember, Jesus said you must know the truth. *You must know it!* When you know it, you can be free, and that means your body, too. You don't have to allow disease and affliction to kill your body. Your body is the house you live in, the temple of God. Why should God want His earthly temple to be diseased with an affliction from His enemy and yours, the devil? (Would you put an expensive new car into an old garage that might fall in on it? Neither does God want His earthly temples to be dilapidated or diseased.)

If your house was damaged and falling in, you wouldn't call

a doctor out to your house, give him some nails and a hammer and tell him to fix it. That isn't his occupation; he probably wouldn't know what he was doing. To get the job done right, you would need to call a professional, like a contractor or carpenter, and have him repair your house right and build it up strong.

The same is true with the body you live in. God made your body, so He's the One best qualified to take proper care of it. As the Creator, He knows everything about every part of it.

Although many doctors are very dedicated to their profession, they're still limited. They know only so much about the different parts of the human body and how each functions. It might take them some time to really diagnose an affliction; and when they do find the problem, it could be too late.

But God knows everything about that infirmity, and your faith in Him can bring a cure. To begin with, He spoke every part of your body into existence. It's no great job for Him to give out a little power to repair it. His supply of knowledge and power can never be used up.

This promise from Jesus is made to you if you'll only believe: **...all things are possible to him that believeth** (Mark 9:23). Speaking through His servant, He said, **Of a truth I perceive that God is no respecter of persons** (Acts 10:34). That means God has no pets, no favorites.

A Living Sacrifice

Remember Paul said in Romans 12:1, **I beseech you therefore, brethren ...that ye present your bodies...** You are the boss, the custodian, the manager of your house. How is your body to be presented? As **...a living sacrifice.** That means total consecration and dedication.

This can't be done if your body is sick or diseased, because it has little life in it to present as a living sacrifice. Paul went on to say that the body should be **...a living sacrifice, holy, acceptable unto God, which is your reasonable service.** God is reasonable.

So present your body as a living sacrifice. Get involved with a good fundamental church that teaches the *full* Gospel, from Matthew through Revelation. That's God's way. Live holy, as Paul says. That's the only acceptable way. Take an active part in spreading the Gospel of Jesus Christ.

Put Jesus first in your life and all the promises of the New Testament (the New Covenant) are yours on this condition: that you serve Him, not only with your words but with your body. As Paul says, this is your reasonable service. God doesn't expect more of us than we're qualified to do, but He does expect us to do all that we're qualified for.

Religious leaders have often said, "It doesn't make any difference what the body does, or even how it sins. The body is never going to get to heaven anyway."

But I declare to you, on the authority of God's Word, that it *does* make all the difference in the world to God concerning what you do with or to your body. He wants your body transformed (renewed and changed). He wants it to be a living sacrifice and holy before Him. This is the only plan or way that's acceptable to Him.

The Holy Spirit lives in your body after you accept Jesus as your personal Savior, and God wants your body to be a house the Holy Spirit can live in. Would you want to live in a filthy, dirty house? Of course not! Neither does the Holy Spirit want to live in a sin-sick house.

Don't ask your body anything. The desires of your body can't be safe to rely on. They might suggest the same life and habits that you had in the past, or even new habits. Those same temptations and weaknesses can come on you, and your body will want to yield to them, so you can't afford to ask anything of your body (your fleshly self). You have to seek God's face and find out what He wants you to do. Don't yield in any way to carnal desires. If you do, your body will rule over your spirit—the inward man—and your spirit man will go down in defeat.

Your faith in God's Word will not only heal you but will keep you strong. Claim the Scriptures God has given you for a well body and stand secure on His promises. Heaven and earth may pass away, but His Word will never fail. (Matthew 24:35) Claim those promises now!

Your Faith Must Take Precedence Over Your Senses

One morning I received a call at my home from a family I was acquainted with. The wife was very sick. She said, "My body is full of pain. It's so messed up. I wondered if you would come and pray for me."

That day I was so rushed and had so many things on my mind that I forgot to go to their home. Then as I was driving along, the Spirit of the Lord suddenly came upon me. He said, "You didn't go pray for that woman!" So I turned my car around at the next side road and went straight to her house.

When I walked in, I saw that she was obviously a very sick woman. She was almost dead with pain. She said, "I went to the doctor yesterday but found no relief. I'm supposed to go again today."

"Well, you don't have to go back," I said. "In fact, it won't be necessary."

"But, Brother Norvel, you don't understand. I have such awful pain in my body. I must get help."

"Jesus is your Help; He's your Relief," I said. "I'm going to break that power over you in Jesus' name and make it leave you."

"But you don't know how bad I'm hurting," she said.

"Don't ask your body anything; in other words, don't look to that pain—look to Jesus."

So I took authority over that pain and disease in Jesus' name. I broke the power that was making her suffer. Placing my hand on her head, I commanded it to go in Jesus' name.

Immediately, God's healing power began to flow through her body. His mighty power made her shake as it surged through her being. Jesus healed her right there as she stood on the floor of her den, and her husband was witness to her healing.

It's impossible to keep your healing when you yield to the symptoms of your body, so don't ask your body anything. In other words, don't yield to the five senses, especially the pain. Look to God's Word and what it says. Stand steadfast with unwavering faith and command the oppressing powers to leave in Jesus' name. When they go from you, God's power will minister to you. You may feel the manifestation of healing in your body as it flows through you, or you may not. We walk by faith, not by what we feel or see (2 Corinthians 5:7). God will heal you when you believe His Word.

It was a pleasure to watch God heal that lady. God's healing power is so precious. **All things are possible to him that believeth** (Mark 9:23).

Now remember, don't ask your body how it feels or what it thinks. Rely only on what God thinks and says. When your life gets all straightened out with His will and His way, healing will be yours!

3

Make Up Your Mind To Be Healed

One time as I was getting ready to speak at a convention of the Full Gospel Business Men's Fellowship in Canada, God's presence filled my room. I had planned to share my testimony about being baptized in the Holy Spirit, and then give an invitation for people to receive the Holy Ghost. But I found out the Lord wanted to teach something else before that.

Jesus said these words to me: "After you are introduced, I want you to teach first what blind Bartimaeus did to get Me to heal him."

When I heard Him tell me that, I gained new respect for healing and faith. Very often, a person will search out new churches to see what God will do for him, to see *if* God will heal him. Jesus wanted me to emphasize what blind Bartimaeus did to get his healing. He was healed on his faith.

To find out exactly how blind Bartimaeus was healed, we need to look at what he did. When you study the Bible, you need to find out what it *actually* says, not what you think it says.

And they came to Jericho: and as he went out of Jericho with his disciples and a great number of people, blind Bartimaeus, the son of Timaeus, sat by the highway side begging.

And when he heard that it was Jesus of Nazareth,

he began to cry out, and say, Jesus, thou son of David, have mercy on me.

And many charged him that he should hold his peace: but he cried the more a great deal, Thou son of David, have mercy on me.

Mark 10:46-48

Jesus gave me a specific order by telling me to teach what blind Bartimaeus did. Actually, Bartimaeus did two things: he asked for healing, then he thanked God for it.

Ask To Be Healed

The first thing blind Bartimaeus did was to cry out. That's the opposite of wondering, as many people do, whether God is going to do something for you. Scripture says he began **to cry out, and say ....** I want you to notice the first word that came out Bartimaeus' mouth: *Jesus!*

Look at the ministry of the disciples who walked with Jesus: **And many charged him** [Bartimaeus] **that he should hold his peace** (Mark 10:48). The people around Jesus didn't believe very hard. Blind Bartimaeus couldn't afford to listen to them. If he had, he would never have received his sight.

The people who go to your church may have all kinds of ideas about what the Bible says. You can't base your beliefs on them. You have to believe the Bible 100 percent! If people believe only 90 percent of the Bible, the remaining 10 percent will rob them.

The second thing blind Bartimaeus said after calling out for Jesus was, **Have mercy on me!** Jesus loves to hear words like that. They get His attention because He's so full of love and compassion.

I've never known Jesus not to respond to any human being as long as that person had even a little bit of faith, even if he was lying in a gutter somewhere. It doesn't matter whether he's black or white, rich or poor, the biggest sinner or the best Christian in town. I've never heard of anybody crying out for mercy and having Jesus turn His back on him. Jesus will *always* respond!

People tried to get blind Bartimaeus to be quiet, but he cried even louder. This shows why 99 percent of Christians don't receive their healing: either they don't cry out at all or they cry out only a few times.

I've had to learn some of these things the hard way. If you don't watch yourself, the devil can attack you with some affliction that's hard to get rid of.

Sometimes I take a thirteen-member team into a church to train the members in how to take the salvation message door-to-door. When I was raising up one of these teams in a church in Mississippi, the devil hit me with weakness and a fever so bad that perspiration was running off my nose. I prayed, but the more I prayed, the worse it got.

By the third morning I was so sick I could hardly walk, so I decided to rest. But as the day went by, I got even worse. By late afternoon, I just wanted to die and go on to heaven.

The devil said to me, "You'll have to get someone else to speak at church tonight. You feel so bad, you can't even get dressed."

Sometimes the devil gets himself in trouble by talking too much. From the natural standpoint, my body was too sick to go anywhere, but when I heard that, I got mad at him for trying to bombard my mind. I jumped up, screaming, "Satan, you're a liar! I'm going to church tonight!" So I ran to the bathroom, jerking off my clothes as I went, jumped in the shower and let the water hit me right in the face.

I said, "Satan, I'm taking a shower and getting ready to go to church because Jesus is my Healer. My body is healed, in Jesus' name!" Then I just kept repeating those words.

The split second I got out of the shower, all those symptoms disappeared. I felt God's power go through me from the top of my head to the bottom of my feet, and I was totally healed! I came out of the bathroom feeling like a sixteen-year-old.

Be like blind Bartimaeus: Don't have any quitting sense and don't waver.

If you feel so bad that you can hardly stand it, just lie on the floor in your own living room and cry out to God for mercy and healing. Cry out (for hours if necessary) that Jesus is your Healer, and God's healing power is for you.

Sometimes I've felt so bad that I couldn't do anything, but I cried out until God's power went through me and totally healed me.

I guarantee that when you cry out as blind Bartimaeus did, with no quitting sense, you'll get heaven's attention. We see in verse 49 that blind Bartimaeus got Jesus' attention, because **Jesus stood still.** Then in the same verse it says **Jesus commanded him to be called.**

> **And they call the blind man, saying unto him, Be of good comfort, rise; he calleth thee.**
>
> **And he, casting away his garment, rose, and came to Jesus.**
>
> **And Jesus answered and said unto him, What wilt thou that I should do unto thee? The blind man said unto him, Lord, that I might receive my sight.**

And Jesus said unto him, Go thy way; thy faith hath made thee whole. And immediately he received his sight, and followed Jesus in the way.

Mark 10:49-52

Jesus asked blind Bartimaeus, **What wilt thou that I should do unto thee?** He answered Him, **Lord, that I might receive my sight.**

You may say, "Jesus already knew what was wrong with Bartimaeus, so why did Bartimaeus have to ask Him for his healing?"

James 4:2 says, **Ye have not, because ye ask not.** God wants you to ask.

If you want healing, raise your voice in faith and ask Jesus to heal you. Go to Him like a little child and say, "Jesus, I need a healing." Then confess Jesus as your Healer, and God's healing power will come to you. Jesus said to blind Bartimaeus, **Go thy way; thy faith hath made thee whole** (v. 52). That blind man immediately received his sight.

Bartimaeus' cries to Jesus were cries of faith. God heard the cries of that blind man. He hears our cries. When the cries get His attention, He heals.

Once when I was speaking in Canada, God told me that if one of the people in the congregation—a man in a wheelchair—would cry out like blind Bartimaeus did, he would be healed. I worked with that man for a while, and he began to confess. After he had cried out for about five minutes, God's power suddenly fell on him. He sat in his wheelchair a few more minutes, still crying out; then he got up and walked across that church.

The pastor said, "He's never done that before!"

31

I said, "He's never confessed like that before!"

That man wasn't embarrassed to cry out, and he got healed.

Don't Be Ashamed

You need to be bold and talk your faith, no matter where you are.

One day as I was walking up the steps of an office building, I was hit with a pain in my right knee. My knee suddenly gave way, and I had to hobble to get to the top of the steps. When I made it to the top, I raised my knee, pointed at it and said, "No, you don't, devil! You can't make my knee give way on me. I won't accept this!"

People were walking up and down those steps. I'm sure it seemed strange to them to see a fellow pointing toward his knee and screaming at it, but I wasn't concerned about what they thought. You have to be willing to confess the Gospel as soon as you need it and not be ashamed.

After sitting there for a while, confessing the Word, my knee got normal. On level ground, I could walk just fine. But the next time I started up the steps, my knee caught again. So I said, "No, you don't. God's power is in my knee. I call my knee normal, in Jesus' name!"

That happened every time I walked up steps for the next six months. The longer it went on, the louder I got. I had to boldly obey the Scriptures, even if talking to my knee did look a little strange to other people.

Then one day I walked up some steps and as I got to the top, I suddenly realized that my knee hadn't given way. It was totally healed and has never given way since!

You have to make up your mind that God wants to heal you

and that He honors faith. You have to show the devil that you're going to have what's rightfully yours and not be embarrassed.

I've been set free from all binding spirits that made me ashamed of the Gospel. I'm not ashamed of any part of the Gospel. I'll cast the devil out of a person while standing on the steps of a church if I have to! People look at me as if I'm strange, but I don't care.

You have to let the Holy Ghost change you so that you don't care what people think, then you can be free and as wild as I am!

Sometimes you have to forget about being nice and polite. When I see a person dying with a disease, I don't want to act nice to the devil! When you get tired of him always trying to fasten cancer or some other disease on you or your family, you'll be ready to stand up and take authority over the situation. You'll be willing to talk your faith out loud. Be bold and talk your faith!

Don't care what you look like to other people; just be wild. Most people won't even be wild at home in front of their families. You have to be careful that your pride doesn't let the devil take advantage of you and beat you into the ground. Sometimes you need to be bold and confess out loud. Don't let embarrassment over crying out to God keep you from being healed. You ought to be hungry to obey Him.

It doesn't embarrass me to walk around in front of a congregation for an hour and tell them to say to Jesus, "Have mercy on me." It shouldn't embarrass you to go forward at a meeting and cry out to God to get your healing.

Only Jesus can heal you. No matter what price you have to pay, cry out for mercy in faith. The biggest price you'll pay is hurt pride. Exactly how long it will take you to pay that price and exactly how many cries it will take for you to get healed, no one can say. The main thing to remember is that you have to pass God's test.

Why I Was Led to Teach About Blind Bartimaeus

When I walked into the ballroom at that Full Gospel Business Men's convention in Canada, I had no idea why God wanted me to teach about what blind Bartimaeus did first to receive his healing. All I knew was that I had to obey God.

The ballroom was packed with people that night. I walked up to the platform and sat down in the one chair that was left at the head table. I knew only two or three people on the platform. The fellows sitting on either side of me were strangers. Since the service had already started, I just scooted in without introducing myself.

In a few minutes the master of ceremonies stood and said: "We're going to change the order of the service. Before I introduce our banquet speaker, Brother Norvel Hayes from Tennessee, we're going to hear a testimony from the donut king of Canada about what the Lord means to him."

That man was called the donut king because he owned a donut empire, which sold hundreds of thousands of donuts a day. He was a multimillionaire.

Just then, one of the fellows sitting next to me, a very distinguished-looking man, pushed back his chair and started toward the platform. But he was feeling his way along. That man was blind! I watched for a moment, then I understood why the Holy Ghost had told me to teach about what blind Bartimaeus did to get Jesus to heal him.

After that man had testified and gone back to his seat, the master of ceremonies introduced me. First, I explained what had happened to me that afternoon, then I said, "I'm going to teach you exactly what blind Bartimaeus did to get God to give him his sight." I wanted that blind man to thoroughly understand what I was talking about. As I was teaching, I leaned over from time to time in his direction. I said, "Blind Bartimaeus kept on crying out. He kept on and on and on."

The people in the audience were sitting on the edge of their seats. They were waiting for that donut king to cry out to the Lord and get healed. They wanted him to do that, but he was a man with a great deal of pride. Having millions of dollars won't cause God to do something special for you. Whether poor or rich, you have to obey the Scriptures in the same way if you want to receive from God.

After the meeting was over, that blind man had to be led out. He didn't receive healing because he didn't cry out to God in faith. If he had just cried out to Jesus as his Healer with no quitting sense, he would have been two verses of Scripture away from healing. The Lord Jesus Himself would have restored that man's sight if he had just obeyed God's Word.

God has a great deal of mercy, and He wanted to share some of it that night. He had the power to give eyesight to that blind man. The Spirit of God had told me specifically what to teach because He loved that man and wanted to heal him. Although he was a born-again Christian who loved God, that blind man needed to claim his healing in order to receive it.

Wounded pride is a small price to pay for receiving your healing!

Give God Thanks for Your Healing

After you've cried out to put your faith to work as blind Bartimaeus did, then you can receive your healing by faith in

Jesus' name. Look up to heaven and thank Jesus for healing you. The Bible says, **In everything give thanks** (1 Thessalonians 5:18).

First: Ask God for your healing.

Second: Thank Him for it.

Open your mouth and say, "Father, I'm asking You for my healing, and I'm thanking You for it now. I believe in Jesus' name that it's done."

Close your eyes and tell Jesus that you love Him. Yield yourself to Him. He will give you your healing as a free gift. You may see something that you've never seen before. He will perform operations on you Himself.

You overcome by the blood of the Lamb and by the word of your testimony. (Revelation 12:11) When Jesus heals you, tell somebody about it. Say, "I accepted my healing today in Jesus' name." Even if people don't want to hear it, tell them anyway; it will build your faith.

Before Jesus fed the multitude, as described in Matthew, chapter 14, He let His voice go to heaven and said, "I thank You, Father, for feeding these people and for bringing Your blessings to them" (author's paraphrase). God heard Jesus' voice. When Jesus thanked God, power was released. God performed a miracle and multiplied those five loaves and two fishes to feed more than 5,000 people. (Matthew 14:15-21)

You may say, "But that was Jesus Who did that!" Yes, and you have the same Spirit living in your innermost being that Jesus had in His. That same Spirit goes through your body and wipes out disease. When the disease leaves, you feel clean. God's Spirit is what makes you feel so clean.

Don't forget to give thanks after you've received your healing, when you're strong and healthy. Every morning thank God because your name is written in heaven. (Luke 10:20) Then say, "Thank You, Lord, for Your healing power."

I say this every day, even though I'm not sick. I thank the Lord that His healing power is working in my body to keep it strong and that my body is functioning like it should.

Remember, You're *Already* Healed!

Notice in Galatians 5:1 where the apostle Paul says:

Stand fast therefore in the liberty wherewith Christ hath made us free, and be not entangled again with the yoke of bondage.

You need to stand fast, or steady, in the promises of Scripture verses you read in the Bible. Your body will be made whole if you'll stand without wavering (vacillating or doubting).

Don't get entangled with people's thoughts or with the religious ideas of those who don't believe what the Bible says about the healing of the body. That's just a snare to entangle you.

Your faith can heal you, but your faith has to be based entirely on what's written in God's Word, not on the feelings and opinions of man.

Now let's read verse 36 of John, chapter 8:

If the Son therefore shall make you free, ye shall be free indeed.

The Son will make you free because you believe His Word. The truth is, you are *already* healed because God's Word says you are!

Our Lord took our infirmities, our sicknesses and our diseases upon Himself:

Who his own self bare our sins in his own body on the tree, that we, being dead to sins, should live unto righteousness: by whose stripes ye were healed.

1 Peter 2:24

If you *were* healed, then you don't have to be healed sometime in the future. **Ye were healed** is past tense, which is saying that you are *already* healed. All you have to do is accept it. So do it now!

Accept what God's Word says about healing for your body. As God's power goes through your body, you can receive complete deliverance from the oppression of the devil and be set free. So claim God's Word now. Your faith *can* heal you!

A Woman's Faith Heals Her

I once prayed for a woman who had just about reached the end of her road. Jesus led her to me for help, but I felt I should have the assistance of another man, who was a minister. I was about to go call him when the Spirit of God came on me suddenly. The word of the Lord came unto me saying, "You don't need that minister; you need Me."

"All right, Jesus. I know that, so I'll just go and pray for the woman myself."

I went to her, fell to my knees beside her and began to pray. I'd been praying for only a couple of minutes when suddenly the power of God came on her. It hit her with such force that she rose to her feet rejoicing and shouting. For several minutes, she danced in the Spirit under the mighty power of God. As she did that, she was healed supernaturally—in body, mind and spirit.

Jesus may use you to help pray another person out of the powers of darkness and into His marvelous light. The person who receives God's power usually will have a deep feeling of gratitude for you. Though Jesus is the One Who did the healing, it's only natural for that person to have a high regard for the "vessel" that was used by God.

For this reason, some years later when that woman became seriously ill, I was called to pray for her. She'd been in the hospital for more than two weeks. When friends and ministers came and prayed for her, nothing happened. She had said to her husband, "When Norvel Hayes comes, I'll be healed."

As soon as I got into town, her husband asked if I'd come to the hospital. He said, "She thinks she'll be healed when you come."

I said, "If that's what she believes, she surely will; but it'll be because she trusts in Jesus, not in me."

When we walked into her room, I looked at her and said, "Oh, thank God for your healing!" Because we as believers have the authority, I put my hand on her head and began to pray. I commanded the devil to take his hand and power off her body. I said: "In the name of Jesus Christ, I bind your power, Satan, and I order you to leave this body alone. I'm not asking you; I'm commanding you! Go from her body now, in Jesus' name!"

Then I claimed the healing power of the Lord Jesus Christ, and God's healing power began to flow into her body. In minutes, she was completely healed!

When I had first come into the room she was nearly dead, but God's mighty power began to flow through her body. She lay on the bed quivering under His power as if she'd been shot with a gun. It wasn't long before she left the hospital and was well.

After some time, symptoms began trying to come back on her, and she didn't resist the enemy as she should have. She went to the meeting of a well-known and successful evangelist who was holding a salvation and healing service. While she was waiting in line, the Spirit of God came upon her. Jesus spoke to her and said, "You are healed; you were healed in the hospital room that day."

Immediately her faith began to rise up and she said, "Yes, I'm healed! I *am* healed!" As she began to claim her healing out loud, the oppressing power of the devil left her.

It was thrilling to hear her testimony of what Jesus had done for her. She was healed because she learned to use her faith.

God will set your body, mind and spirit free by His mighty power, and He will do it on a permanent basis, according to your faith. So build your faith on His Word and trust Him now. There's no such thing as failing. Your faith can heal you!

Jesus Talked About Faith

In the Gospels, Jesus talked many times to people about their faith and their believing.

Jesus asked two blind men, "Do you believe that I'm able to do this?" They said, "Yes, Lord, we believe." Then Jesus said, **According to your faith be it unto you,** and the blind men's eyes were opened immediately. (Matthew 9:27-30)

So often the person who is ill wants to put the responsibility onto the one who's praying for him. But in the Scriptures, Jesus shifted the responsibility of believing back to the individual.

Vicarious faith is faith that one person can have for another's needs or healing. Jesus never used His own faith; He always healed according to the faith of the individual He was praying for. The same is true today.

Vicarious faith is necessary when the person we're praying for can't exercise his own faith. Jesus raised the dead using His own faith. But in other instances, He worked or answered according to the faith of the individual.

If Jesus said in the New Testament that your faith heals you, then He's still saying it today: *Your faith heals you!* The price has already been paid. Just accept it now! Your faith is an absolute requisite. *You* have to do the believing, not someone else.

In Luke 16:17, Jesus said, **And it is easier for heaven and earth to pass, than one tittle of the law to fail.** God's Word cannot be contradicted or disproved, repealed or changed. It's easier for heaven and earth to pass away than for His Word to fail. There's no such thing as any part of God's Word failing to him who believes.

Since **all things are possible to him that believeth** (Mark 9:23), this means it's possible for God's healing power to come into your body. God can straighten limbs, open blind eyes and heal any afflictions in your body, regardless of how serious they may be. The mountain of affliction in your body may be too tall to climb over, but you can become tall enough in God's Word to just step over it.

Your Faith Can Make *You* Whole!

Another important Scripture that I want to refer to is Mark 5:28. This scripture is talking about the woman with the issue of blood who was following Jesus:

She said, If I may touch but his clothes, I shall be whole.

Verse 29 says:

Straightway the fountain of her blood was dried up; and she felt in her body that she was healed of that plague.

I want you to notice that: the woman with the issue of blood went to Jesus. So don't wait for Him to come to you. You have to go to Him *through His Word* and *through your own believing*.

Look at what happened when she touched Jesus' clothes:

And Jesus, immediately knowing in himself that virtue had gone out of him, turned him about in the press, and said, Who touched my clothes?

And his disciples said unto him, Thou seest the multitude thronging thee, and sayest thou, Who touched me?

And he looked round about to see her that had done this thing.

But the woman fearing and trembling, knowing what was done in her, came and fell down before him, and told him all the truth.

And he said unto her, Daughter, thy faith hath made thee whole; go in peace, and be whole of thy plague.

Mark 5:30-34

Take special notice of how Jesus said to her, *Thy* **faith hath made thee whole.** Now stop and think: If her faith made her whole, and God is no respecter of persons, then *your* faith can make *you* whole. If it can't, then Jesus loved that woman more than He loves you, and He'd have to be a respecter of persons. But He's not!

Faith Puts God's Love To Work

Jesus loves you just as much as He loved the woman we read about in Mark, chapter 5. He called her "daughter." If you are a born-again child of God, you are His son or daughter. God loves *all* His children the same. His love is great enough, broad enough and deep enough to include all of His children.

Yes, He loves you just as much as He did that woman. God doesn't show partiality; He loves everyone the same. Your faith puts God's love to work, and He works for everybody, including you!

Wouldn't it hurt you a lot if someone you loved doubted your word? Then you can see how God delights in you when you believe Him and accept His Word. **But without faith it is impossible to please him** [God] (Hebrews 11:6). That means it's impossible to find favor in His sight without faith. It's an insult to Him for you to doubt His Word. **Satan is a liar, and the father of it** (John 8:44), but **God's Word is Truth!** (John 17:17.)

Are you ashamed to tell people that Jesus is the Healer? Are you ashamed to study the Scriptures that tell what God said concerning faith? If you *are* ashamed, and ashamed to come to Him, then you aren't going to be healed. Much of what people have been taught is junk because it's only based on man's ideas, but the Truth will triumph over all.

Jesus said, **I am the way, the truth, and the life** (John 14:6). Jesus is the Truth, and there's no other truth anywhere else, except truth that is based on His Word. Any part of God's Word that you deny or are ashamed of is the part you can never have. God, through His Son Jesus, has made it possible for you to be healed.

It's a sad, terrible and disgusting thing then for a believer to have sickness in his body, to be lying flat on his back, just withering away day after day, year after year. What a waste of power—God's power!

God doesn't change. He doesn't fail. He doesn't lie. He doesn't make promises He can't keep!

It simply doesn't matter what people think, not even those closest to you. It's what God's Word says that really counts!

God is counting on you. Why don't you count on His Word? The only part of God's Word that will ever help you is the Word that you know for yourself. This not only means saving words, but healing words. Your faith, being strong enough to believe His Word without wavering, will bring healing to your body.

Die to the Flesh and Live for Him

God wants you to deny your own ways and accept His way. In Luke's gospel Jesus said:

If any man will come after me, let him deny himself [meaning to deny the things your body wants if they're contrary to God's will and ways], **and take up his cross daily, and follow me.**

For whosoever will save his life shall lose it: but whosoever will lose his life for my sake, the same shall save it.

For what is a man advantaged, if he gain the whole world, and lose himself, or be cast away?

For whosoever shall be ashamed of me and of my words, of him shall the Son of man be ashamed, when he shall come in his own glory, and in his Father's, and of the holy angels.

Luke 9:23-26

For whosoever shall be ashamed of me and of my words... This means salvation here, but don't be ashamed of any of God's Word including healing words.

Verse 27 says:

But I tell you of a truth, there be some standing here, which shall not taste of death, till they see the kingdom of God.

When we do God's will, we become subjects of His kingdom, thus an heir of His kingdom. That means heir to all God owns, which includes His healing power for our bodies.

But we have to be willing to deny ourselves to the point that we put His kingdom and the advancement of His kingdom first in our lives, **...and take up his cross daily** (v. 23). Jesus bore the cross, not for Himself or for *His* sins, but for ours. Likewise, if we want to become a key part of His kingdom, we have to be willing to share the burdens and needs of others.

God wants you to "die" now so that you can "live" now. He who loses his life shall save it. So die to your flesh, and refuse to feed your body the things of this world. If you don't, the devil will be able to attack you, and you'll become vulnerable to his tactics.

If you give your body to the devil, he will have the right of way to attack. God doesn't want you giving your energy to some religious organization that doesn't teach the Truth; neither does He want you to give of your time and means to such.

Instead, give *all* of your being to God—spirit, soul and body.

I pray God your whole spirit and soul and body be preserved blameless unto the coming of our Lord Jesus Christ.

1 Thessalonians 5:23

4

You *Were* Healed ...

Some people teach that we don't die until God is ready for us to die. But this idea isn't in line with the teaching of God's Word. It's a lie from the devil! The devil can steal your life early! Now I realize that many who believe this are honest and sincere Christians, but you can still be a Christian and believe what the devil tells you about your body. He will tell you all kinds of things, but only God's Word is the Truth.

My mother and father were honest, down-to-earth, old fashioned churchgoers from Tennessee. They were good Christians. But being a "good Christian" has nothing to do with believing the Bible. My mother died of cancer at the age of 37, and my brother died of Bright's disease at the age of 19. Though healing was for them, they didn't know it. Nobody had told them about it.

I didn't realize it then, but unscriptural praying leaves the door open for the devil to attack your body even though your spirit is in tune with Jesus. The Holy Spirit Who lives in your body works in line with your confession of the Scriptures, and your confession has to be in faith.

My mother loved Jesus with all of her heart. She was always involved at church, praying and working for Jesus. She was always telling people about Him and winning souls for the Kingdom. She was constantly praying for people until they would be convicted of their sins and would give their lives to God. So it didn't make any sense to me that God would kill her at age 37.

When our mother died, I was only ten years old, my sister was eleven and a half and my brother was fourteen. As a cotton-headed boy, I thought that either God killed her or it was His will for her to die. Because she'd always loved and served Jesus, I didn't consider that the devil had anything to do with her death.

While she was ill, people prayed, "Lord, heal Mrs. Hayes, if it be Thy will." What they were actually saying was, "Lord, if it's not Your will to heal her, just go ahead and kill her." I was too young then to understand that kind of praying.

It's horrible when the mother of three young children dies. Those children only have one mother, and they certainly don't want to lose her, so they cry and wring their hands. People are always telling them, "Jesus loves you, and He knows what He's doing."

It's true that Jesus knows what He's doing, but what He was doing had nothing to do with that death. The average Christian is trying to connect something the devil did with Jesus.

In the church where I grew up—the one my mother went to—the people prayed with their lips only. They weren't really exercising any faith. They just said, "Lord, heal Mrs. Hayes if it be Thy will."

But Mrs. Hayes died.

Man's Way vs. God's Way

As a boy, I thought, *Well, it must not be God's will to heal my mother.* I didn't know the Scriptures like James 5:14, 15 which says:

Is any sick among you? let him call for the elders of the church; and let them pray over him, anointing him with oil in the name of the Lord:

And the prayer of faith shall save the sick, and the Lord shall raise him up.

Verse 14 asks, **Is any sick among you?** This Scripture included my mother, but she had never been taught about that. She didn't know to call on the elders of the church and have them bring a bottle of oil to anoint her body and pray the prayer of faith for her.

My mother had never been taught to say with her mouth by faith, "Because God promised me, He will raise me up." She'd never been taught to put her faith in these two verses and trust God for her healing. So she died prematurely.

Some say it was God's will for my mother to be sick and die and leave her family at a time when we needed her so much. But that makes God seem cruel, and God isn't like that. He's a God of love and He loves to heal people. But He can't heal them unless they first believe, and they can't believe unless they read and stand on God's promises.

God demands that His requirements be met, and Jesus demands that the last chapter of the book of Mark be obeyed. He says, **Lay hands on the sick, and they shall recover** (Mark 16:18). That's God's way.

Man's way says, "It's okay to pray a little prayer—but don't ever lay hands on anyone!" That's the reason people are in trouble and why so many die before their time.

God not only promised health but in the Old Testament, He promised long life to those who obey His laws and believe His Word.

If you have much knowledge of the Bible at all, you know that the New Testament is an even better covenant to live under than the Old Testament. We're living under the New Testament that has even greater promises than the old one. It has easier instructions to follow and shows us how we can receive power from the spirit world, where God is the boss. That power is available so that we'll be able to help ourselves and our fellow man.

I didn't know these truths at the time my mother died. I learned them later, but it wasn't until after another tragedy had struck our home.

When my brother died at age of nineteen, I thought the same thing about him that I had about my mother: it must have been God's will for him to die too. People prayed the same way: "Lord, heal Glen Hayes if it be Thy will." But we buried him. I didn't know then that the Scriptures were life for the human body.

After I grew up, and received Jesus into my heart and began studying the Bible, I found out that kind of praying for the sick is caused by doubt and unbelief, and it isn't scriptural. In John 10:10, Jesus says plainly that the devil is here for three reasons: to steal, and to kill, and to destroy. Jesus today is just like He is in the New Testament, and He never killed anybody.

God's Explanation to Me About My Mother's Death

After I turned my life over to God, I still didn't know it was the devil who had taken the life of my mother and brother. So for three days, I sought God in prayer, particularly concerning my mother's death. I'll explain a little later what I received from the throne of God on my third day of prayer.

First, let me remind you again: God didn't put these Scriptures in this chapter for just a few people. He's trying to explain to you (through the Bible): **My people are destroyed for lack of knowledge** (Hosea 4:6). (See also Proverbs 29:18) This means that people are destroyed for the lack of knowledge of what God's Word actually and literally says. If people don't have the knowledge that it is God's will to heal them (through going to a church that teaches the Bible or through reading and studying God's Word themselves), the devil can kill them with sickness and disease! God wants us to be informed so we can live an abundant life!

After I got into the business world, I was very successful and my business grew. At the end of the month I liked to see credits instead of debits on my profit-and-loss statement. The same thing applies to the spiritual realm.

I couldn't find any place in the New Testament where God put diseases on His children. If I hired an employee and he was a good one, I promoted him. God does the same thing with His children. If we stay in line with His Word, we'll enjoy the benefits thereof.

So as I was seeking the Lord in prayer for some answers about my mother's death, I said:

"Jesus, I don't want to pray wrong, so if I'm out of line, forgive me. Being a businessman who likes credits instead of debits, it really makes no sense to me why You killed my mother. To You, one soul was worth more than the whole world, and my mother was winning souls for the Kingdom. But You killed her when she was only 37. If You had let her live to 65 or 75, she would have won a lot more souls."

"I don't want You to get angry with me, Jesus, but it doesn't make sense to me why You took my mother and brother. I just don't understand. Please tell me why You did it."

On my third day of prayer, the Lord began talking to me about this.

You may say, "I wish God would talk to me that way." If you pray long enough, He will. Had I prayed for only two days to find out the answer, I still wouldn't know why my mother died; but after I'd prayed long enough, the Lord answered me.

Very plainly, God said, "Son, I didn't kill your mother; I didn't have anything to do with it."

That statement was a shock to me.

"Well, if You didn't have anything to do with my mother's death, then why did You let her die? She didn't want to die. She loved You; she was a Christian."

Then He said this:

"I tell you in My Word that death is My enemy. I don't go around putting sicknesses and diseases in people's bodies; the devil does that. I didn't put those tumors in your mother's body; the devil attacked her. Those tumors killed her, but they didn't come from heaven; there's no sickness here to be given out."

"I tell you in My Word that all good things come down from heaven. Your mother could not receive divine healing for her body because she didn't know how to receive it."

"Remember, son, people can't believe something they haven't been taught."

"That's right, Lord. People can't believe something they haven't been taught."

Jesus told me why my mother wasn't healed. It was because of where she went to church. He said: "Your mother could not receive My divine healing power because her church did not teach the people how to receive their healing. People only receive what they are taught how to receive."

My mother didn't know how to receive God's healing power for her body. She had never been taught how to receive it. She had never been taught to obey the healing verses in the New Testament. Those promises don't work automatically; they come through faith in God's Word. God *is* the Word, God *was* the Word, and God will *always* be the Word. God and His Word are the same.

God's Will Is Healing

All the teachings of the New Testament and the provisions that have been made in heaven for the human race are for everybody. People can't enjoy the provisions God has made for the human race unless they believe. They can't believe unless their faith in the Scriptures is strong.

It isn't good enough to try to build your faith on what you've been told. Maybe you belong to a church that doesn't obey certain Scriptures. For instance, in chapter 16 of Mark's gospel Jesus said, **Lay hands on the sick, and they shall recover** (v. 18), and James 5:14 says, **...anointing him with oil in the name of the Lord,** so that God's healing power can be imparted to the sick. If your church doesn't obey such commands, you need to find a church that teaches the *full* Gospel (the Good News) of God's power.

While I was growing up, I never saw these Scriptures practiced. I saw people get saved and join the church, but I never saw any faith being put into the verses that called for the healing of the body. As the Lord later showed me, no human being can jump over the Word, believing only what he wants to believe, and still receive all of God's benefits.

God is the Truth, and there is no other. He wants you to open your ears and let your heart be receptive to His promises. If you'll put your trust in what God says, your faith can heal you. The Bible says, **So then faith cometh by hearing, and hearing by the word of God** (Romans 10:17).

The Prayer of Faith

Jesus will heal people only one way—through faith—and He will heal anyone who trusts Him.

You might ask, "What is faith?"

God's Word says in Hebrews 11:1, **Now faith is ....** If it's not *now,* it's not faith, and it doesn't work! **Now faith is the substance of things hoped for, the evidence of things not seen.** You can't wait until you've seen a disease healed before you believe God's Word.

You have allowed your life to be bound up in too much natural bondage in your own way of living that it's hard for you to understand the ways of God. You should have been feeding your faith with God's Word. But if you haven't, it isn't too late. You can return to His Word now and fling yourself on it for deliverance.

Your faith in God's Word will heal you only if you act upon it. If you haven't really trusted in God's Word in the past, just repent now and tell Jesus you're sorry. Then start studying the Scriptures on healing and begin to claim them for your body.

Begin saying with your mouth: "I accept God's healing power for my body, and I believe I'll receive what I pray for. I realize, Jesus, that You love me as much as You loved that woman in the fifth chapter of Mark's gospel. She had been suffering for years, but when she reached out to You for healing, You gave her what she was believing for."

Either you'll get your thinking straightened out by God's Word or you won't receive. You aren't going to make God do anything, but your faith in the Scriptures can heal you. Yes, it is God's will for your body to be healthy.

Now the Bible teaches us how to pray for the sick. Let's look again at James 5:14, 15:

> **Is any sick among you? let him call for the elders of the church; and let them pray over him, anointing him with oil in the name of the Lord:**

> **And the prayer of faith shall save the sick, and the Lord shall raise him up; and if he have committed sins, they shall be forgiven him.**

It's just as easy for Jesus to heal as it is for Him to save. Many people have been raised up from a bed of affliction through the anointing of oil and the prayer of faith.

In Mark 11:24, Jesus said, **What things soever ye desire, when ye pray, believe that ye receive them, and ye shall have them.** Not maybe, not sometimes, but *every* time. Not later, but *now—when you pray.*

"They Shall Recover!"

In Mark 16:17, 18, Jesus gave the believers His Great Commission (or command) concerning the work He was leaving for the Church. He said what He wanted *every* born-again believer to do, commanding them to **....lay hands on the sick, and they shall recover** (v. 18).

This command concerning the sick and their needs wasn't given only to ministers; it was given to *every* believer. Jesus' promise is: **They *shall* recover.**

Absolute Protection for Those Who Trust in God

God has promised health and healing, protection from disease and victory over the enemy. He also has promised constant divine protection. Let's look at these promises from His Word:

He that dwelleth in the secret place of the most High shall abide under the shadow of the Almighty.

I will say of the Lord, He is my refuge and my fortress: my God; in him will I trust.

Surely he shall deliver thee from the snare of the fowler, and from the noisome pestilence.

He shall cover thee with his feathers, and under his wings shalt thou trust: his truth shall be thy shield and buckler.

Thou shalt not be afraid for the terror by night; nor for the arrow that flieth by day;

Nor for the pestilence that walketh in darkness; nor for the destruction that wasteth at noonday.

A thousand shall fall at thy side, and ten thousand at thy right hand; but it shall not come nigh thee.

Only with thine eyes shalt thou behold and see the reward of the wicked.

Because thou hast made the Lord, which is my refuge, even the most High, thy habitation;

There shall no evil befall thee, neither shall any plague come nigh thy dwelling.

For he shall give his angels charge over thee, to keep thee in all thy ways.

They shall bear thee up in their hands, lest thou dash thy foot against a stone.

Thou shalt tread upon the lion and adder: the young lion and the dragon shalt thou trample under feet.

Because he hath set his love upon me, therefore will I deliver him: I will set him on high, because he hath known my name.

He shall call upon me, and I will answer him: I will be with him in trouble; I will deliver him, and honour him.

With long life will I satisfy him, and shew him my salvation.

Psalm 91

In these Scripture verses, God has made promises to those who'll trust Him completely. He has promised refuge and protection; prosperity (protection from pestilence that destroys crops); freedom from fear; protection from the robber and thief; protection from demon forces (**those that walketh in darkness** -v. 6); protection in battle (**A thousand shall fall at thy side** -v. 7); victory over enemies; even the attention and divine care of His holy angels (v. 11).

In verses 15 and 16, God promises deliverance from trouble and the right to call on His name at any time, as well as honor and long life. What more could anyone need?

Fear and trouble can put people in the hospital and even drive them insane, but that isn't God's will for the human race. Many people live in constant fear, so great that their lives become a burden. Jesus came to break that bondage.

You need to claim all the promises in Psalm 91, and you need to confess them out loud. Believe them first; then the manifestation (or proof of His power) will come.

All of God's promises are conditional. If we abide under

the shadow of the Almighty (Psalm 91:1), we're living close to Him.

Jesus Gave You Power Over the Enemy

And Jesus came and spake unto them, saying, All power is given unto me in heaven and in earth.

Go ye therefore, and teach all nations ...whatsoever I have commanded you: and, lo, I am with you alway, even unto the end of the world. Amen.

Matthew 28:18-20

Don't worry about Jesus leaving you. Don't worry about God's healing power not working for you. Jesus plainly said He had all power in heaven and in earth, so His power is available here on earth, and *it's available* to *you!*

Jesus Christ is the indisputable Victor: **And having spoiled principalities and powers, he made a shew of them openly, triumphing over them in it** (Colossians 2:15). **Death is swallowed up in victory** (1 Corinthians 15:54). To believers, He said: **... because I live, ye shall live also** (John 14:19) and, **Behold, I give unto you power to tread on serpents and scorpions, and over all the power of the enemy: and nothing shall by any means hurt you** (Luke 10:19).

All the power of the enemy includes power over sickness and disease, over sin, and over the enemy of our soul—the devil. This authority has been given to *every* believer, without reservation.

The Price for Healing Was Paid by Jesus

The same God Who spoke the world into existence, the same God Who spoke the parts of your body into existence, the same God Who gave His authority to His believers will also speak and bring health back to your body. Believe it now! Accept it by faith. Confess it with your mouth out loud!

Again, notice Matthew 21:22 where Jesus said, **And all things, whatsoever ye shall ask in prayer, believing, ye shall receive.** He said **all things** (in line with His Word). I repeat, *all things!* Believe *now* as you ask for it. Don't waver in your faith. (To waver is to be tossed back and forth between two opinions or forces.) Don't be tossed and torn by the two forces of belief and unbelief. Don't waver. Don't fear. Don't doubt. Just believe!

James 1:6 says, **But let him ask in faith, nothing wavering. For he that wavereth is like a wave of the sea driven with the wind and tossed.** God's Word is your compass. You need to be secured and established in His Word.

You can get up off the bed of affliction by God's power. God loves you, and He wants you to receive that power. He wants you to accept it now! Start talking faith. Start talking what you believe. Start talking what the Bible says. You're healed because the Word says that you are! So start talking health.

The price for healing has already been paid, just as the price for salvation has been paid. That price was paid by Jesus as He bore the stripes in your place. (Isaiah 53:5) It's yours to accept or reject. So don't let the devil steal from you through wrong ideas. If you base your belief on opinions or feelings, there's little hope for you to recover now or ever.

As Jesus bore that cruel beating in Pilate's hall, you were healed. This was prophesied of Jesus Christ:

> **He was wounded for our transgressions, he was bruised for our iniquities: the chastisement of our peace was upon him; and with his stripes we are healed.**
>
> **Isaiah 53:5**

When Jesus came to earth, He fulfilled that prophecy. He drank the bitter cup of suffering down to the last dregs of pain, and even to death. Why? So that you might be free from sin, that you might have peace, that you might be healed.

Notice that healing was the first provision Jesus made for your redemption. He was beaten *before* He was crucified, and by those stripes you were healed. He died for your sins, but He was beaten for your sicknesses.

You were healed includes you! So believe it, say it, and act upon it! Do this now, and the victory *will* be yours!

5

Faith At Work!

I have a personal friend who was born premature, weighing less than two pounds. Parts of his body were deformed because they had never developed, and his blood wasn't right. The doctor didn't expect him to live past his teenage years.

My friend grew up in a Christian home. But when he went to church, the only subject he ever heard preached was salvation. He was taught the way of salvation through faith in the Lord Jesus Christ, but he didn't know or understand about divine healing through the power of God. Sometimes he attended another denomination, but divine healing wasn't preached in that church either.

With this lack of knowledge about the healing of his body, my deformed friend had suffered all his life. To the doctors, his case was absolutely hopeless; they'd never seen anyone in his condition live past sixteen years of age.

By the time he was a teenager, he was bedfast and was just withering away. It seemed that death was very near. It was almost impossible for him to carry on a conversation, as he would stammer and stutter so. His case was pathetic indeed.

My Friend Desired To Be Healed

With all hope in the ability of man's skill completely gone, my friend turned to God's Word for comfort. He asked for a

Bible and began reading it.

Since he was paralyzed and almost blind, he could only read for a short time each day. He began with the first book in the New Testament, the gospel of Matthew. After several days when he had finished Matthew, he began reading in the book of Mark.

He was attracted by a particular verse that he found in the eleventh chapter of Mark's gospel. In verse 24 Jesus said:

> **Therefore I say unto you, What things soever ye desire, when ye pray, believe that ye receive them, and ye shall have them.**

When he read this verse, hope began to rise in his heart, and he read it over and over again. Finally he said:

"Jesus, since You haven't told a lie in this verse, I'm coming out of this bed. You said, **What things soever ye desire**, and I desire to get up from here. You know I desire to go to heaven, but I also desire to have a well, strong body like other boys. You said I could have what I desire, so I'm going to pray and I'm going to believe and I'm going to receive."

Eleven months went by, and nothing happened. My friend waited night after night for God to come and heal him, but it didn't happen. Why? Because he didn't know how to release his faith.

Discouragement Came

My friend was desperate, so he asked for three different ministers to come to his house. He wanted to know if Jesus really meant what He said in Mark 11:24. After several days, only one of them came to see him.

When that minister went into the young man's room, he

was shocked at what he saw. The boy was almost a skeleton, over six feet tall but weighing only eighty-nine pounds—just skin and bones. It seemed that he soon would be taking his last breath. The boy had been lying there for sixteen months, just holding on day after day, reaching out for just a straw of hope.

Stammering and stuttering, my friend tried hard to ask the minister about Mark 11:24, but words just wouldn't come. Thinking the boy couldn't talk, the minister patted his hand and said in a sober, pious voice, "Just be patient, my boy. In a few days it will all be over." Then the minister turned around slowly and walked out of the room.

To my friend, that minister had put out the light of the little ray of hope that he had. This only added to his discouragement, leaving him more depressed and confused than ever. It seemed so dark in that room; all the light he had hoped for had been put out. (My friend still weeps whenever he tells about this.)

The minister walked out into the living room and began praying for the family. He asked God to be kind to them and to give them comfort in their time of grief at the inevitable death of their loved one. Hearing that minister praying from the other room, my friend wanted to scream out, "But I'm not dead yet! Do you understand me? I'm not dead yet!"

After the minister left, the relatives came into the room and asked, "Son, what kind of flowers do you want for your funeral?"

My friend only stuttered, "It doesn't make any difference; I won't be able to see them." *

Then they asked, "Who do you want for your minister and pallbearers? And what songs do you want sung?"

"It doesn't make any difference; I won't be able to hear them anyway."

In the conversation between the minister and those relatives, they almost had my friend buried, and he was still breathing! But they promised him a good funeral.

The way of man isn't the way of God. The ways of man will put out the light of your hope many times, especially if you're deformed or afflicted with an incurable disease. In that case, you can't look through the natural eyes of man; you have to look through the eyes of God and behold the light of His Word.

The best and most qualified doctor in the land can look at you and say, "There's no hope." The most qualified minister (at least from an educational standpoint) can look at you and say, "There's no hope." Yet, right in the middle of all that, God's Spirit can shine through that dark cloud of hopelessness with God's Word that says, "By His stripes you are healed."

Faith Requires Some Action

All the darkness in the world can never put out the light of that one little candle. Neither can all the doubt in the world stop your healing from taking place if you yourself don't put out your ray of hope in God's eternal Word by unbelief.

The Bible teaches that **faith without works** (or action) **is dead.** (James 2:17) You have to understand this and keep it in your memory forever.

My young, deformed friend had to learn the lesson of active faith before he could be healed. The Word of God is carried to our heart and spirit by the power of the Holy Ghost. The Holy Ghost—the Third Person of the Godhead —is here to help us, and He was there to lead my friend into the truths of God's Holy Word.

My friend then began to read in the fifth chapter of Mark, where the Holy Spirit opened up another divine secret to him. He read how the woman with the issue of blood said, **If I may touch but his clothes, I shall be** [made] **whole** (Mark 5:28). He read how that woman forced her way through the crowd in her weak body, but with unwavering faith to receive what she so desperately had to have. He read how by her own effort she touched Jesus' clothes and released her faith. Immediately Jesus rewarded her faith by allowing His healing virtue to flow into her body. (It only took one touch from Jesus!)

As my friend read this story, his faith began to rise again. He realized that he had to put forth a natural effort to act upon God's Word because that faith without works is dead. Slowly he began to see that he could get a miracle in his life, but he had to use his own faith, not someone else's, and he had to put forth some action himself.

You see, faith must have action mixed with it. Faith without action is dead! You have to believe it's true. You have to say it's true. You also have to act like it's true. God doesn't tell lies. His Word isn't a book of fiction. He doesn't make up stories for entertainment. He means business!

If you really mean business and really want healing, not just sympathy, then follow these three simple steps: Believe! Say! Act!

Active Faith Brought Healing

As my deformed friend began to understand the truth of active faith, he started moving by faith. He took his elbows and pushed one paralyzed leg off the side of the bed. But it hit the floor like a chunk of wood! He then reached over with his elbows, wiggled around and pushed his other leg off the bed.

It also fell like a chunk of wood. There was no feeling in either of his legs.

With much effort, he worked around and finally mustered enough strength to push his body off the bed and onto the floor. His body fell with a thud! Still, nothing happened.

He began making his way to the foot of the bed with his elbows, dragging his dead body along. Locking his arms around the foot of the bed, he said:

"Jesus, You said in Mark 11:23 that we can have what we say. If I don't doubt You in my heart, anything I say will come to pass. I can have *whatever* I say."

"You said in Mark 11:24, **What things soever ye desire, when ye pray, believe that ye receive them, and ye shall have them.** I believe in my heart that You've heard my prayer. I believe that I've received healing for my body, so I'm saying it with my mouth."

He then began to scream out loud: "Mark 11:24 is mine! I believe I have my healing! I believe I'm healed because Mark 11:24 says I am. I confess with my mouth that it's mine now! I've got it! I confess this before God, in the face of the devil, and in front of anybody who asks me: The contents of Mark 11:24 are mine! Thank God for a well body! Thank You, Jesus, that Mark 11:24 is mine!"

While he was screaming this, my friend said it was as if someone was standing over him and pouring warm honey out of a jar. He said it tasted sweet as it was going down through his body. It seemed to be slowly running down his face. When it ran over his eyes, he could see well!

It went down through his neck and into his shoulders, then down through his body. When it came to his heart, a new heart popped into his chest! The organs that had been deformed in his body straightened out and became perfect.

Then as it went down into his waist, feeling came into his body down through his paralyzed legs. His legs became strong and straight as feeling and life came back to them!

As it went out his feet, he had feeling and perfect blood throughout his body and all the parts of his body were restored to normal!

He stood straight up in the middle of the floor and walked—and he's been walking ever since! He tells people that Jesus healed him, and he isn't ashamed to give his testimony to anyone, anywhere.

It's so important that we confess our salvation and our healing before man. The Bible teaches that we overcome by the blood of the Lamb and the word of our testimony. (Revelation 12:11)

For this reason, and to encourage others to believe, my friend tells people the good news of God's healing power everywhere he goes.

Believe, Receive, Act

But you have to remember that the contents of Mark 11:24 aren't just for my friend. If he hadn't firmly stood on those promises, he would have died long ago. Likewise, many hopeless cases will soon die unless they learn these great scriptural truths and believe and act upon them, just as my friend did.

My friend wasn't willing to take no for an answer, and we don't have to take no for an answer either when God is saying yes. But remember, you have to say yes too. "Yes faith" connects you with omnipotence and channels you into the miracle world of heaven's power.

Jesus said, **What things soever ye desire, when ye pray, believe that ye receive them, and ye shall have them.** *Ye* means Y-O-U! That means you who are reading this book! Believe right now, and you will be set free from the bondage of Satan.

Jesus said, **All things are possible to him that believeth** (Mark 9:23) and, **Ask, and it shall be given you** (Matthew 7:7). God's Word also says, **Ye have not, because ye ask not** (James 4:2).

So ask God right now for your healing. Begin to thank Him out loud for the answer to your prayers, regardless of what it is. Whatever the need may be, God will answer if you're asking in His will—and it *is* His will for you to be healed.

Thank God out loud for the answer right now! Praise Him! The doctor may have told you that your disease is incurable and that you will die soon, but you don't have to die.

Don't Let Satan Steal From You

Let me give you a word of warning right now: Satan will come and try to steal God's Word away from you. That's one of his favorite tricks. He will work hard to get you so involved with other things and the cares of life that he will take God's Word from your mind and lips. He will even try to put pain and symptoms back in your body to get you to doubt your healing.

Satan is a poor loser, and he will continue to lose as long as you'll keep looking to God's Word and quoting those promises out loud and thanking God for your healing.

God's Mighty Power

God's healing power is strong and mighty, and it's available for the human body so that it can be healed and then used to pray for others.

Some time ago as I was sitting close to a crippled woman, I saw her get healed by God's mighty power. She just got up out of her wheelchair and started walking. As she went back to the ambulance that brought her there, she was pushing the wheelchair she'd been wheeled in on!

Seeing all that just made me break down and begin to cry. I wasn't weeping because I was sad; I was weeping because I'd been so touched by the love and power of God and what He had done in performing that great miracle. Oh, God's power is so sweet, so real, so strong, so wonderful!

Don't let Satan steal that beautiful power from your body. It's the manifestation of God's divine presence in your life. It crushes and defeats the the power of Satan—the power of sin, the power of his disease, the power of his fear.

You no longer have to be a slave to sorrow and sickness. No wonder Satan tries to keep you from believing the Word! He hates you because you're God's child. He can't strike back at God or even touch Him, because Jesus destroyed his works and became the uncontested Victor. So he keeps striking back at God's children. God's Word, His power and Jesus' shed blood are your shield. So use them against Satan's attacks.

Power Over the Devil

God is now pouring out His Spirit upon the earth and revealing His Word to His people like I've never seen before. As we're obeying Jesus' command that was given in

Mark,chapter 16, we're taking authority in the name of Jesus Christ, commanding the devils to leave the bodies of those they've been tormenting.

Often I would come to a person who had been sick for a long time and whose body (and sometimes mind also) had been attacked by the devil. I would take authority over that power of darkness. As I broke it in Jesus' name, the demons would get mad. They'd come out screaming in anger, because they had to leave through the power of that name.

Demons are evil spirits that need a human body to dwell in and torment. They're such hateful spirits. They can only be happy and satisfied when they're tormenting the human race— God's creation. They violently hate God's people. They want only to destroy us and take us with them to their last and final home, the lake of fire. (Revelation 21:8)

Demons are powerful beings, but we as believers have been given the authority over them in Jesus' name. Thank God, many of us are taking that authority! As believers we don't have to fear them, but we must fear sin.

God is unfolding and revealing His Word to us today in such a beautiful way for the salvation of the lost, the sick and the weak. But let me warn you: we have to live holy lives and not let Satan steal God's Word from our hearts. That would make us helpless to the attacks of the demon world with its sin, sickness and disease.

Not only will Mark 11:24 work for you, but so will all the Scriptures throughout the New Testament. Satan tries hard to prevent people from reading their Bible and going to church where the full Gospel is preached. When people do finally hear the truth, the devil will come and try to steal away the Word they've heard. As Jesus said, when the sower sows the

Word, Satan comes immediately to take away the Word that was sown. (Matthew 13)

Satan has no defense against the Word of God. He has no defense against the lordship of Jesus or the name of Jesus. He has no defense against the born-again believer who's walking right, living right and acting on God's Word.

Jesus said, **All power is given unto me in heaven and in earth** (Matthew 28:18). Satan has been stripped of his powers, and Jesus has turned those powers over to the Church. When you were born again by the Spirit of God, you became a part of that great Church. It isn't found in any one denomination; it has been given to every truly born-again person who will accept that power and use it to God's glory.

The True Bible-Believing Church

Jesus said to His followers, **I will give unto thee the keys of the kingdom of heaven** (Matthew 16:19). But these "keys" of faith and His Word, and faith in that Word, will do us no good unless we use them.

As a part of His great Church, let's use the keys of the kingdom. If we build the Church that Jesus wants built, it won't be a church that believe only part of the Bible and denies the rest; it will be a church built upon His Word —*all* of His Word.

When Jesus went away, He left His authority to the Church. Now I'm not speaking of a church that doesn't believe in divine healing, casting out devils, the baptism in the Holy Spirit or being saved (born again) by God's Spirit. I'm speaking of the true Church that believes the whole Bible, whatever it says.

God's power is only available to that kind of church—the Bible-believing church. People in church who don't believe in these divine truths of God's Word are only "playing house" with all of their rituals and ceremonies.

Satan doesn't fear that kind of church; he only laughs at it. But he's afraid of the true Church: where divine authority in God has taken over his kingdom of darkness, where diseases are healed, where demons are cast out, and where people get saved and quit the sinning business once and for all.

God's business is the most important business on earth. He left His disciples (His followers) in charge of it. His business is to break the power of Satan over people's minds, bodies and spirits; then they can become fit subjects of God's kingdom.

A Sick Church

If it's the most important business on earth, then why do so many so-called ministers of the Gospel either neglect it or ignore it? Why do they give first place in their churches to the doctrines of men with all kinds of programs which don't further God's Word? Why have they allowed Satan to sidetrack them from the real purpose of the ministry and the responsibilities of believers to carry out the Great Commission of Mark 16? We have to see an old-fashioned returning to all of the Word of God!

You see, the devil would like people to stay satisfied and content and set in their own ways. He operates like this many times through the Church. Things that seem right and look good and appeal to most people are often only devices, like "wolves in sheeps' clothing." That's a deception of Satan.

Denominations that grab hold of such ways have no real power of God to deliver a lost world out of Satan's hands. They've turned into moral social orders, and sometimes not so moral. That means they're only social orders, nothing more than a friendly club. That's a sick church, and it needs healing itself before it can help bring deliverance to a lost and dying world.

One person can't deliver another person from bondage if he's in bondage himself. He has to first break his bonds through faith and belief in God's Word. Until then, he can never be qualified to break the bonds of others. One blind man isn't qualified to lead another blind man; they both will fall in a ditch. Only God's Word can cure that blindness!

Some church people only believe part of God's Word. *The part you don't believe is the part you can never have!* Why not believe it all? Why not believe and enjoy the full benefits of Calvary? They were all purchased by Jesus' own stripes and by the shedding of His own blood. Why cheat yourself?

The basic principle of the Christian life is to know that God put sin, sickness, disease, sorrow, grief and poverty on Jesus at Calvary. For Him to put any of this on us now would be a miscarriage of justice.

Jesus, Who was sinless, was made a curse (willing to become sin) that we might receive all the blessings of Abraham, the father of the faithful. Glory be to God forevermore! Jesus died for the whole human race. Then He willed His righteousness and authority over to us. All we have to do is just take it! So take it by faith, in Jesus' name.

A Divided Kingdom

As James 1:8 tells us, **a double-minded man is unstable in all his ways.** A double-minded man is like a person trying to ride two horses at the same time; he will eventually be torn asunder. This is the mental state of those who are double-minded. They're trying to serve two masters at the same time, and they'll be tom asunder, too.

If a man is double-minded, he will fall. If he imagines, assumes, or in any way has the idea that God is behind his troubles, then he never will resist Satan.

Jesus said:

> **And if a kingdom be divided against itself, that kingdom cannot stand. And if a house be divided against itself, that house cannot stand.**
>
> **Mark 3:24, 25**

If God delights in the afflictions of His people and brings them on His followers, who make up His kingdom spiritually, then God is divided against Himself and His kingdom cannot stand. But God's Word tells us that His kingdom will stand forever.

Sickness, fear and sin are tools of the devil. God doesn't stoop to use the devil's tools against us. God's kingdom is a kingdom of love, joy and peace in the Holy Ghost; Satan's kingdom brings torment. The devil is a warped personality. He's twisted and crazy in his thinking, and he wants his subjects—his followers—to be just like him.

Satan has absolutely no authority whatsoever against God's eternal Word, and he knows that. But as long as he can fool you and talk you out of believing God's Word and acting on it, he will be able to keep you from victory.

God doesn't use Satan to discipline His family!

Suppose your child disobeyed you to the point that discipline was needed. Would you do it yourself in love as it should be done, or would you allow some evil person to come in and chastise your child by beating him or her in line? The answer is obvious.

What is the chastisement of the Lord? Does God use Satan to punish His family? If you study the Old and New Testaments about this subject, you'll find that God never put sicknesses on His children.

There were a few times, however, when He allowed Satan to put afflictions on them, as in the case of Job. This was to test Job's integrity with God. But God never allowed the affliction to stay on him; He turned it into a miracle. God proved to Satan that Job was righteous. He proved that Job would remain true to Him under all circumstances.

God has the power to heal the afflictions of the devil; or in other words, He has power and authority over the devil. Satan accused Job before God, saying that if God would take the hedge from around Job, Job would curse Him to His face. But God proved Satan out to be a liar through the faithfulness of Job.

Our faith in God and His Word will always prove Satan to be a liar. God doesn't afflict His children. I repeat: sin, sickness and fear are tools of the devil, and God will never stoop to use Satan's tools.

If you've been afflicted by the devil, maybe it's because God has been bragging on you. But remember, you don't have to keep that affliction! God will turn it into a miracle right now by healing you, and your testimony can help others.

Be Filled With Divine Power

God wants your body to be strong so that you can serve Him and be a holy vessel with His divine power flowing out through you to help others.

Get involved in a good Full Gospel church. Begin to study God's Word so that you can then teach it to others. Give your life as a living sacrifice, holy and acceptable to do God's service. Give of your money to the Lord to help proclaim the full Gospel (Good News) of the Lord Jesus Christ. Then, most of all, get filled—and stay filled—with God's Spirit as we're told to do in Ephesians 5:18 and First Corinthians 12:13.

Take the Gospel of power and life and deliverance to the sick and the dying. Be filled with the Holy Ghost as the early Church was, then you'll be empowered from on High to do God's work and undo Satan's work.

John the Baptist said:

> **I indeed baptize you with water; but one mightier than I cometh, the latchet of whose shoes I am not worthy to unloose: he shall baptize you with the Holy Ghost and with fire.**

> **Luke 3:16**

And Jesus said:

> **But wait [tarry or seek] for the promise of the Father, which, saith he, ye have heard of me.**

> **For John truly baptized with water; but ye shall be baptized with the Holy Ghost not many days hence.**

> **Acts 1:4, 5**

Then Jesus gave the reason for such a mighty baptism of His Holy Spirit, which was to follow John's baptism in water— the baptism of repentance. Jesus said:

> **But ye shall receive power, after that the Holy Ghost is come upon you: and ye shall be witnesses unto me both in Jerusalem, and in all Judaea, and in Samaria, and unto the uttermost part of the earth.**

> **Acts 1:8**

There it is in simple language. The purpose of the Holy Ghost is for you to receive power from God and be witnesses. You'll be very limited as to what you do for God's kingdom until you receive that power. It's available for every believer and for those willing to take time out and seek it.

"It Is Written..."

Now back to the main theme of this chapter: you too can be healed of your diseases, regardless of how serious they are. You can become a great witness for God just as my young, deformed friend was. God can turn that curse into a blessing, but you have to believe His Word and act on it, just as my friend did.

God works through faith, and there's no other way on earth that He can work! He demands that we have faith in His Word in order for us to get our prayers answered.

It's an insult to God for us to doubt His Word. You are healed because the Bible says so. No other reason is necessary. It's already written and it can never be changed. God provided healing for you. He wants you to be well and happy.

Tell the devil that you're believing God, because *It is written,* just the way Mark 11:24 states it.

Repeat these words out loud: "I have what I prayed for and I prayed for a well body. I'm already healed! I accept it in Jesus' name, because it's written that way."

You do this, and Satan has to leave you. He can't fight God's Word. He can't stand before God's Word. He can't defeat you as long as you're acting on God's Word.

Remember, stand on God's Word. It is written by God. Your faith in God's Word can heal you! That's your faith in action!

The number one way for you to receive your healing is by faith in God's Word. But there are several other ways you can receive God's healing power. These other ways can be found in God's Word. In the next few chapters we'll take a look at what God's Word says about each of these scriptural ways for healing.

6

Jesus Heals Through
the Laying On of Hands

In these verses from Mark's gospel, we can see an example of how Jesus healed by laying hands on people. It says:

There came a leper to him, beseeching him, and kneeling down to him, and saying unto him, If thou wilt, thou canst make me clean.

And Jesus, moved with compassion, put forth his hand, and touched him, and saith unto him, I will; be thou clean.

Mark 1:40, 41

Notice how the leper came to Jesus for healing. He humbled himself before the Lord by kneeling down and making a statement of his faith. That incurable disease had broken out all over him, but he knelt down before the Lord and said, "Jesus, You can make me clean." And Jesus was moved with compassion.

Jesus is the same yesterday, and today, and forever (Hebrews 13:8). He has never changed. His compassion has never changed. So you can come to Jesus the same way that leper did, and He will heal you, too!

One night I was holding a meeting in Atlanta, Georgia, and the Lord said to me: "When a sick person comes sweetly to the altar, as that leper did to Me, kneels down before Me and says,

79

'I've come to receive my healing, Jesus,' My heart goes out to him. My love and compassion flow out to him."

As Mark's gospel tells us, Jesus put forth his hand, touched that leper and said to him, **Be thou clean.** And that leprosy departed immediately! (Mark 1:41, 42)

Doctrine of the Laying On of Hands

Laying hands on people is a doctrine of the New Testament Church.

In this passage from Mark chapter 16, Jesus tells the believers to continue His ministry:

> **And he said unto them, Go ye into all the world, and preach the gospel to every creature. He that believeth and is baptized shall be saved; but he that believeth not shall be damned.**
>
> **And these signs shall follow them that believe; In my name shall they cast out devils; they shall speak with new tongues.**
>
> **They shall take up serpents; and if they drink any deadly thing, it shall not hurt them; they shall lay hands on the sick, and they shall recover.**
>
> **So then after the Lord had spoken unto them, he was received up into heaven, and sat on the right hand of God.**
>
> **And they went forth, and preached everywhere, the Lord working with them, and confirming the word with signs following. Amen.**
>
> **Mark 16:15-20**

Much of the ministry in the New Testament is through the laying on of hands.

In verse 16, what is he that believeth believing? Jesus is

talking about the Gospel. The whole New Testament is the Gospel: salvation, healing, miracles, laying on of hands, and special miracles through handkerchiefs and aprons.

Verse 15 states the Great Commission of the Church: **Go ye into all the world, and preach *the gospel* to every creature.** From verse 18 we see that part of the Gospel is the laying on of hands. Going into the world and preaching the Gospel to every creature means preaching about the laying on of hands.

If you go to church where ministers don't lay hands on people, that church isn't obeying all of the Gospel. Being obedient to the Gospel includes the laying on of hands.

When you preach about this doctrine, then you should do it: lay your hands on a sick person; God's power will heal him!

Jesus Commissioned *All* the Church

The laying on of hands is for *all* believers and *all* churches. The casting out of devils is for *all* believers and *all* churches. You just have to learn how to do it.

Sometimes ministers will call me and say, "Brother Norvel, the Lord wants me to go on the road with you. I'll pay my own way." They go and stay with me two, three, maybe four weeks, and just watch me pray for sick people and cast out devils.

After seeing the way Jesus gently works to heal people, they take what they've learned and go back to their own churches. When they start obeying the Scriptures themselves, God changes their whole church.

Learn To Lay Hands on the Sick

One time when I was speaking at a banquet in Georgia, six pastors who came to that meeting had never before experienced healing in their ministries. During that time, God proved to them that He heals people through the laying on of hands.

The banquet room where we met was packed. While I was speaking that night, the Lord moved on me to say this to the audience: "If Jesus has never physically healed anybody through your hands or in any other way through your ministry, I want you to come and stand before me. The Lord wants me to say a prayer for you."

Those six ministers came up. After asking them what denominations they were from, I said, "All of you are pastors of Bible-believing churches. Do you believe in the triune Godhead?"

They said, "Yes."

"Do you believe that Jesus died on the cross for you, that He rose from the dead, that He's sitting on the right hand of the Father, making intercession for the Church, and that the Bible is true?"

"Yes."

I told them to stand around me; then I put my hands on theirs and prayed for them.

I said:

"Father, these men are Your chosen vessels. They're called to preach the Gospel and to bring people into heaven. I ask You now to put in their hands the same anointing of healing power that You've put in mine. Anoint them with Your healing power. Let it flow from my hands into theirs right now. I thank You, Father, for doing it. I claim it to be so, in Jesus' name."

I was acting on directions straight from heaven.

Then I said, "Now we're going to see miracles and healing power come into this place."

I had all the sick people come and stand across the front of the room. Then I divided them into six sections. I told each of those six ministers to take one of the sections and lay hands on those people. I said: "Instead of praying a long prayer, just gently lay your hands on the people and say, 'In Jesus' name, receive your healing.' Watch what God does; then go on to the next one."

The ministers did what I told them to do. Suddenly the healing power of God came on one person and caused him to drop to the floor. The pastor who prayed for that person was amazed as he looked down at his hands.

Those six pastors prayed for everybody in that ballroom. By the time they had gotten through the first healing line, they were weeping. Looking at their hands, they said, "I can't believe this is happening to me!"

When everyone had been prayed for, I then gave some instructions to the pastors. I said to them:

"Don't be ashamed to have healing lines in your own churches. Educate your whole congregation in one service. On a Sunday morning tell your people, 'Jesus loves you. He wants to save you and all your relatives, and He wants to heal you. Jesus is your Healer.'

"Then read Mark 16 and say to them, 'God gives me an order here. He says for me to lay my hands on sick people. Because God loves you, He wants to heal you.'

"Call your people up and say to them, 'I'm going to do what Jesus Christ tells me to do. I'm going to lay hands on you and tell you to receive your healing, in Jesus' name.'

"As you go down the line gently and quietly, the Lord will heal people, and your congregation won't be offended."

To get God to work for you, you have to obey Him.

Learn To Cast Out Devils

As we read before, Mark 16:17 says, **And these signs shall follow them that believe; In my name shall they cast out devils; they shall speak with new tongues.**

People say you ought to love first. You definitely need to know the love of God, but you also need to know your duties as a Christian. The first two things in the Gospel that you should do are throw out the enemy and talk in a language that drives him nuts.

You can be a good Christian without casting out devils. Many Christians don't cast out devils, even though Jesus tells us to do it. But if you don't cast out devils and speak in new tongues, you should start. The Church needs to learn how to fight the enemy by casting out devils in Jesus' name.

Sometimes I'll go to a church and ask, "How many people here cast out devils?" Hands will go up all over the audience.

Other times when I ask that question, people just look around instead of raising their hands. Even if they do cast out devils, they don't want to admit it.

If no hands go up, I say, "Jesus wants me to ask you another question: When are you going to start?"

Then everything gets real quiet. That doesn't go over too well, but I don't want it to. I deliberately try to make that kind of church nervous.

The Gospel was written by God to jar people's thinking.

You need to think scripturally; God doesn't want you to think like you normally do. You can have a church without casting out devils or speaking with new tongues, but it will be a weak one. You have to take authority over your enemy, the devil. You have to pray in tongues, or his demons will know what you're going to do, even before you do it. Don't be ashamed when you cast out devils and pray in tongues.

Delivered and Set Free!

One time as I was speaking at a Sunday morning church service, the Lord showed me that there was a homosexual in the congregation. The church was overflowing with people that day. There were about two hundred visitors. So I was going to be nice and wait until after the service, then take that young fellow over to the side room and cast the devil out of him.

When I had finished speaking and had given the altar call, I prayed with those who came up to the front. The Spirit of God was moving so sweetly and blessing the people when the Lord said to me: "I want My ministry out in the open. Side-room ministries don't please Me as much as altar ministries. I want you to cast the devil out of that boy so that the church can watch."

I went over to that fellow, who was about sixteen years old, and had him stand up. Whispering in his ear, I said, "I know you're a homosexual, but I won't let the congregation know about it. I'm just going to cast that spirit out of you right now. You want to be free, don't you?"

"Yes," he said.

Then I spoke directly to that spirit. I said: "You foul spirit, in Jesus' name, I take authority over you and command you to let go of this young man! I break your power now! You have to obey me and come out of him. In Jesus' name, you can't have this young man. He belongs to God because I say he does.

"Satan, God made this body and you can't have it! This body belongs to God, and I command you to obey me. I take authority over the foul spirit that's trying to wreck this young man. Turn him loose now!"

I stood there, calmly speaking those words, repeating them over and over again.

All of a sudden that thing broke loose and came out of him. God's power began to shake him so hard that I couldn't hold onto him. Then it knocked him flat on his back. He lay there quivering, crying, rejoicing and thanking the Lord. Later he said to me, "I wanted so much to be free!"

The people in that church loved God. After they saw such a demonstration of the Holy Ghost, they couldn't keep from rejoicing. Nobody there knew that young man had been delivered from homosexuality; it was none of their business. But they could see that he had been set free because of the way he was rejoicing.

Jesus loved that young man. He wanted him to be set free from homosexuality. To be free, you need to have patience and not be ashamed of the Gospel, even if it means being delivered on a Sunday morning in front of the whole church and two hundred visitors! Because I obeyed the Gospel and cast the devil out of that boy, he was delivered and set free!

When Praying for Someone in a Mental Institution

To help a demon-possessed person, you have to do certain things. Take, for instance, people in mental institutions. If you're asked to go and pray for someone in a mental institution, you should do it only if God gives you instructions. You won't accomplish a thing if the Lord doesn't tell you to go.

First, you have to bind up the devil in Jesus' name. In Matthew 12:29, Jesus said to **bind the strong man**, which means the devil.

Second, you should pray in the Spirit for God's will to be done for that person. Praying in the Holy Ghost will cause God's will to be performed. There are some things we just aren't smart enough to figure out and pray about in English. We aren't smart enough to know the different things that need to be prayed for concerning some people, but the Holy Ghost is! That's why we need to pray in the Spirit.

Third, when that person finds enough freedom, get him to start confessing that he's free.

Doing these three things will bring anybody out of a mental institution.

God Confirms With Signs Following

You have to learn what God's Word says, then do it. When you do God's Word, you become established and your faith gets stronger. Then you'll know your rights in Christ Jesus and know that the Lord Jesus will do anything for you when you only believe His Word.

God will confirm His Word with signs following. (Mark 16:20) After you obey God by laying hands on the sick, He will heal them. When you cast out devils in Jesus' name, those devils have to leave.

Tell the Truth

Sometimes when a pastor takes me out to eat after church,

our conversation goes something like this:

"Brother Norvel, I wish I were like you. I want to say some of the things you say, but I'm afraid to. I don't want to make my people mad."

I always answer by saying, "Don't be afraid; just spit it out. Your people may get mad, but they'll get over it."

If you haven't been in the presence of God often enough for Him to share much with you, then you won't have much to minister to other people. But once God shares things with you, you have to share those things with others, even though you may not want to. People will never get ministered to if you don't tell them the truth.

Sometimes a person won't believe the Word of God at first, but later he will remember it and believe it, even if he heard it six months before. When God says to do something or say something, don't try to figure out why—just do it!

You should always tell the truth. Church should be a place where you learn about life and find out what God has for you, not a place where everything is kept secret. Churches should hold sex classes for young people and teach them exactly what to expect when they get married (and to wait until they get married).

Sometimes you have to blast people with the Scriptures for them to believe it. In my meetings, some people sit half stunned when I tell them that the Spirit of God will heal them and put their homes back together. They think, *I'm not believing my ears.* But when I blast them with the Word, God does it!

One night when I gave an invitation, God told me to pray individually for the people standing in line. He said, "Take authority over the devil. Then agree in My name with each person for his need. As the two of you agree together, My power will begin to work for that person."

So I took each person by the hand and asked, "What do you want from the Lord?" Then I ministered the way God had told me.

One of the people that came forward was a pretty brunette about twenty-eight years old. She said: "Brother Norvel, Jesus told me that if I'd come up here and tell you about my problem, you could tell me what to do. I've never told anybody about this before. My problem is that I don't want my husband to touch me. I don't let him. I can't stand for him to."

"How long have you been married?" I asked.

"About three years."

"Did you have sex with him on your honeymoon?"

"Yes."

"Wasn't it sweet?"

"Yes, it was. But after we came back home, something took me over and I can't stand for him to touch me. I don't know what to do. I just can't talk about it to anyone at church."

I hate the devil! It would take the devil to have a warped mind like that. God wants a husband and wife to be one, but the devil wants them to be two.

As I took her hand, I spoke right at the devil. I said, "Devil, I break your power over this girl. I command you to take your hands off her marriage, off her husband and off her body. I command you to set her free so that she can be a normal wife. She has the God-given right to be loved by her husband and to enjoy life to the fullest. She has a right to join with him and be one flesh with him forever. You're not going to steal from her! In Jesus' name, set her free!"

Then I told her what to do. I said, "My sister, you're free now. Do you believe it?"

"Yes," she said.

"Then you have to put action to your faith. When your husband tries to touch you, I want you to make yourself respond to him. You may not want to, but do it anyway. First, make up your mind that you *can* do it; then do it!"

Jesus blessed me for ministering to that girl and her husband. I've seen them several times since then, and God has done a real work in their lives. He has given them three children.

Almost every time I go to that city, I see that precious family sitting in the congregation. One time I was able to visit with them in their home.

When I first walked into their house, her husband said, "Brother Norvel, let's all hold hands and pray. The Lord used you to save our marriage, and we want you to ask Him to continue His blessing. For the first three years of our marriage, this house was cold and dead, but you told us the truth and this has turned into a warm, sweet, beautiful home that's full of love."

As we stood there holding hands, the Spirit of the Lord swept in and swallowed us up. We just broke into weeping and rejoicing.

Don't be afraid to tell the truth!

God wants His tender love to flow in every room of a Christian home, and you can experience that love in your own family. Married couples must never allow the devil to rob them of their pure, sweet love and the special moments they share as husband and wife. Don't let it happen! Claim your rights in Christ and refuse to let the devil rob you.

Straighten Out Your Thinking

God is waiting for you to get your thinking straightened out so that He can bless you. It makes no difference how smart you are; it's what you do with the Gospel that counts.

A Spirit-filled teacher invited me to speak at Southern Illinois University where 22,000 students were attending at the time. The university had made a rule that there would be complete freedom of speech and press. For students to hear a wide variety of views, the classrooms were turned over each night to different organizations. In one classroom there was to be some teaching about witchcraft; in another room, people were putting on a homosexual play.

When that teacher heard about it, he asked if there could be a meeting about Jesus in one of the classrooms. After he got permission, he invited me to come there and speak. He said, "Brother Norvel, would you be willing to come and teach the Bible right next door to where they're having a homosexual play?"

I said, "Praise God, why not?"So I taught there for a week, and a big crowd came.

One night I asked the audience, "How many of you have seen Jesus heal people?" Hands went up everywhere.

"I'm going to pray for the sick tomorrow night, so you can come and watch God heal people all over this place."

The next night, I prayed for the sick by the laying on of hands. I had people come up on the stage. Even though it was ten times as big as a regular stage, there wasn't enough room for everybody.

After coming to that meeting, a patient of the school psychiatrist told him about it. He said, "This Norvel Hayes doesn't talk like a normal man; he talks wild! But I've been listening to him, Doctor, and my mind has cleared up! I've been coming to you for years and have paid you a lot of money, but in just two or three days, I've gotten help! Brother Hayes takes authority over devils. You need to go hear him talk about God!"

The psychiatrist said, "He takes authority over devils? If this Norvel Hayes is as wild as they say he is, I might as well go hear him."

I had been holding morning and evening classes every day, so the psychiatrist came to a morning class. After the service, he called where I was staying and left a message for me to call him back. When I did, he said: "Mr. Hayes, I've never before heard a human being talk like you. I don't know anything about what you were saying, but somehow it made sense to me. I need to talk to you. Would this afternoon be convenient?"

When we met, the first thing he said to me was, "My mind is telling me that all the things I've heard you say just aren't true."

"I understand that, Doctor, but I'll help you now. Pull all that education out of your brain and lay it on the table. [That education, for the moment, was making him put his faith in all he'd learned about the natural realm.] Believe the Bible, trust God and listen like a little child. Let me reason with you. I can talk to you for an hour and still have two hours before service time. Ask me any questions you want. If I can't answer them, we'll look them up in the Bible; God has the answer in His Word."

He agreed.

"Doctor, I know why you can't believe what you've heard me talk about. As a psychiatrist, you tell people how to live, but you haven't learned how yourself. You leave your office, go to the country club, have cocktails for an hour or two, and then go home. You've been doing that for years. But now you find yourself wondering about things. You look at the bottom of that cocktail glass and you think, *I spend all day teaching people how to live, but I don't know how myself. Are cocktails and country clubs all life has to offer?*"

"How did you know that, Mr. Hayes? I've thought that many times, especially during the last few years. I've sat there wondering that very thing, *Is this all God has to offer, a cocktail party at the country club after work?*"

"Sure, you've thought about that, Doctor. Everything in the world gets old after a while. It has nothing to offer. It's all phony. But Jesus and the Holy Spirit don't get old. They're for real! I've already been where you are, Doctor. But the Lord will make a new human being out of you and set you totally free."

After we talked for about an hour, I said, "Will you come tonight, Doctor? It's the last meeting."

"I wouldn't miss it!" he said.

That night I gave the congregation a double dose. I spoke first on healing—how to receive the power of God to get your body straightened out—and then on the baptism of the Holy Ghost.

When I gave an invitation for healing, I said, "If you want to be healed, come stand in front of me so that the Lord Jesus can heal you. He's the Healer, not me."

The psychiatrist was the first to come forward. Because Satan had caused physical problems in his body, he didn't just casually get up—he jumped out of his seat! Then some other people came and stood.

I said, "All you people who need more power from God, get up out of your seats and stand on the other side of the room away from these who have come up for healing. Jesus will give you more power."

Then that psychiatrist said in a loud voice, "Mr. Hayes, is it all right if I leave this line and get over there in the other one?"

The whole crowd laughed.

"Take it easy, Doctor. You're too anxious."

"But I want more power!"

"Just take one thing at a time. Let the Lord heal you first, then you can get in the other line to receive power."

I prayed for the people in the first line and laid hands on them. When I'd finished praying for the psychiatrist, I said, "The Bible says you're healed, Doctor."

"I am?"

"Yes, you are. Now you can go stand in the other line so you can get more power."

Just a few minutes after I prayed for him again, he was talking in tongues!

After listening to me and watching me for only two services, he began ministering to other people. He told them how Jesus would heal them and give them power; then he invited them to his home. People started getting healed and baptized in the Holy Ghost.

After I had left town, he called to tell me what was

happening. He said, "Prayer meetings are getting so large that I can hardly get all the people in my house! I cast out devils just like you did. I say, 'In Jesus' name, come out!' I lay my hands on the sick and claim their healing in Jesus' name, just like you did, and God heals them."

The next year, I was asked to come back to that university and hold meetings for two weeks. During that year, the psychiatrist had led his family to God.

His wife was an alcoholic, but after my first meeting there, he went home and told her that God had healed him and baptized him in the Holy Ghost. When she saw how well he was, she said, "If you can get something from God, I surely can."

God saved her and baptized her in the Holy Ghost; then He saved their daughter. That family got turned on to God! All of them took part in prayer meetings, praying for people and casting out devils.

According to the psychiatrist, his daughter had gone from being "way out in left field" the year before, to being probably the strongest Christian in town. When God manifests Himself like that, it will get you straightened out.

When I asked the psychiatrist why his daughter's faith was so strong, he said: "She saw what God did for her daddy and mother. When I prayed for sick people, she saw Jesus heal them. She believes God can do anything.

"One time when she and her husband were walking in the country, a child fell in a well. The wall of the well was too high for them to reach down and grab the child's hand, and they couldn't find anything big enough to step on to reach the child. So they cried out, 'God, help us!'

"Suddenly they saw a big rock by the well that hadn't been there before. God had created that rock in response to their prayer! By stepping on that rock, they were able to rescue the child."

When I went to speak at the university that next year, I met the psychiatrist's family and was invited to their home for a meal. I could see that his wife and daughter were totally dedicated to God. Talking doubt couldn't shake the daughter. (If God made a rock for you, wouldn't you believe He could do anything?)

Remember, the psychiatrist was a highly educated man. When he learned to obey the Gospel, God healed him and abundantly blessed him.

Once educated people see the truth in something, they will believe it. I've won more medical doctors to the Lord than any other profession. God gives me favor with them. When I pray for doctors, God usually heals them. Then they put healing Scriptures all over their office walls. God also gives me favor with chiropractors.

When I was speaking at a Full Gospel Business Men's convention in Memphis, Tennessee, I met a chiropractor and his wife. They went to a denominational church, so they had never been to a meeting like that one before. I was scheduled to hold a three-day meeting at a church in Kentucky when the Memphis convention was over. It happened that they lived only forty miles from there, so they asked if they could drive me to that meeting.

I had already made arrangements for the pastor of that church to pick me up in Memphis, but when they asked me to ride with them, the Spirit of God said, "Go with them."

On the last day of the convention in Memphis, the pastor

called my hotel room to find out what time I wanted to leave. I told him what the Lord had said for me to do and that I would be at his church in time for the service on Sunday night.

When the chiropractor and his wife drove me to that church, I said, "Why don't you stay for the service?"

He said, "Do you think it would be all right? We've never been to this kind of church before."

"It will be fine. You can go as my guests. I'll get seats for you up front."

That night after I had taught on healing, I said, "If you believe Jesus is your Healer and you want Him to heal you, come up here."

As soon as I said that, the chiropractor jumped out of his seat and came forward. I laid hands on him and said, "Thank You, Jesus, for healing him." Immediately he was knocked back by the power of God, and he fell flat on the floor. When his wife saw that, she came up and the same thing happened to her. The Holy Ghost healed both of them right there.

After that, he became a member of a Full Gospel church and later an elder. Since then, I've seen the two of them giving their testimony on television. He said, "We didn't know Jesus healed today until we went to a church service with Norvel Hayes. He taught on healing, and then he prayed for us. Jesus healed both my wife and me of diseases we'd had for years!"

7

Jesus Heals Through the Head of the House

As we saw before, Hebrews 11:1 says, **Now faith is the substance of things hoped for, the evidence of things not seen.** Your faith is your *own* substance and your *children's* substance. Your children aren't capable of believing very much unless you've taught them the Word of God from the time they were little.

My daughter, Zona, was healed, but it wasn't at a church or in a healing service. She was healed at home, and her faith had nothing to do with it. She was healed through my faith and my confession. I confessed a verse of Scripture for forty days before her healing manifested. She said that during all that time my confession was driving her nuts.

Seeing My Daughter Suffer

Zona's body was covered with boils, knots and ugly warts that started appearing when she was eleven or twelve years old. I took her to a doctor and they were removed through surgery, but the knots came back and brought their cousins with them! By the time she was fifteen or sixteen years old, she had forty-two growths on her body.

By that time, I had been baptized in the Holy Spirit and was trying to pray and believe God for her healing. But the more

99

I believed God, the bigger the knots seemed to get! Zona's healing didn't manifest because I was ignorant.

After I had prayed for three years, the devil began to bombard my mind with worry.

When Zona started dating, it was embarrassing for her. She didn't have trouble getting dates, but she would say to me, "Daddy, it's embarrassing for me to date. I hate it when boys want to hold my hand. My hands are so ugly!" She wanted her hands healed so much that she called the doctor herself about having the knots removed again.

I was trying to study faith and learn how to confess it, but something wouldn't let me. I kept backing away from it.

About that time, Kenneth Hagin and his wife were passing through town so they stopped to stay a few days with me. When they got to my house, I was at my office so they went to my neighbor's home and called me. As soon as they called, I went over there. The last time the Hagins had been in town for a meeting, those neighbors had fixed dinner for us.

We all were sitting in their den talking when Zona and their daughter came in from school. Zona hadn't seen the Hagins for several months.

Brother Hagin said, "Zona, how are you doing?"

"I'm doing just fine, Brother Hagin, except that I'm having trouble with my dad. He won't do what I want him to."

"What do you mean?" he said.

"Look at my legs and knees. See how ugly they are? They've got knots all over them. The doctor said that if I'd come to the hospital for one night, he'd put me to sleep and take off all those growths at one time; then I'd be free of them. But Daddy won't let me! I've been asking him for a year, but he keeps saying he'll think about it. Will you talk to him?"

Then Brother Hagin said, "Zona, I can curse those things and they'll disappear."

When he said that, everything got real quiet. I looked over at the lady of the house and saw how uncomfortable she was. What was I supposed to do? Brother Hagin would be leaving in a few days, but I had to live next to those people! Changing the subject, I said, "The weather in Tennessee is really nice this time of year."

I had worked with Brother Hagin and I knew him well enough to know that he was telling the truth, but I didn't know what he meant when he said, "I can curse those things." I knew how to pray for the sick, but I didn't know what he was talking about. He said it in the same way he would have said, "I can go to the store with a dollar and buy a loaf of bread." He said *he* could curse them.

I had always thought Jesus was supposed to do everything. Zona was a good Christian and loved the Lord, and I knew Jesus loved her. But I had been raised in a church where it was taught that if you loved God, He would do something for you—if He wanted to. So I thought God would heal Zona only if He wanted to.

I intended to ask Brother Hagin what he meant when he said he could curse those growths, but when we got home we started talking about other things and I never thought about it again. Later, I wondered how I could have forgotten something like that. I forgot because God blocked my mind, and I realized later why He did—He wanted to tell me the answer Himself.

Learning My Responsibility
As Head of My House

About two weeks later, I was walking through the house after a Sunday evening service. Zona was sitting in the den with her boyfriend. I had no earthly idea that anything unusual was about to happen to me. I was just walking through the living room thinking about how Brother Hagin could curse growths.

All of a sudden, my natural senses were put on hold. I was caught up into another world and God began talking to me. I'd seen the Lord once before, but in this particular manifestation I just heard His voice. When God talks to you, it's not the same as when human beings talk to you.

He said, "How long are you going to put up with those growths on your daughter's body?"

God will put up with our diseases as long as we will. When I had the flu, He put up with it for three days because that's how long I did. When I got tired of putting up with it, I jerked my clothes off and jumped in the shower. Even though cold chills were running all over me and I was having hot flashes, I stood there with water hitting me right in the face and I screamed out that I was healed.

When God asked me how long I was going to put up with those growths, I was ignorant of my rights in Christ Jesus and I was scared, so I answered, "But they're not on me, Lord! I don't have them, Jesus!"

When I said that, I found out how shocked the moneychangers must have been when Jesus ran them out of the temple. (Matthew 21:12,13.) Without wasting any time, God told me, "You're the head of your house!"

Then He said: "You belong to me just like Kenneth Hagin

102

does. You don't need him to pray for your daughter. You can curse those growths in My name just like I cursed the fig tree. If you believe and don't doubt, they will die and disappear."

The passage of Scripture the Lord used with me was Matthew 21:19-22.

> **And when He [Jesus] saw a fig tree in the way, he came to it, and found nothing thereon, but leaves only, and said unto it, Let no fruit grow on thee henceforward for ever. And presently the fig tree withered away.**
>
> **And when the disciples saw it, they marvelled, saying, How soon is the fig tree withered away!**
>
> **Jesus answered and said unto them, Verily I say unto you, If ye have faith, and doubt not, ye shall not only do this which is done to the fig tree, but also if ye shall say unto this mountain, Be thou removed, and be thou cast into the sea; it shall be done.**
>
> **And all things, whatsoever ye shall ask in prayer, believing, ye shall receive.**

Notice in verse 21 He says, **If ye have faith ....** You must have faith and doubt not.

God isn't the head of the house; the man is. God told me to curse those growths because I was the head of my house. When He told me that, I saw something most fathers have never seen: The things that go wrong in a man's house are his own fault.

If a child has been sick for two years, it's not the child's fault or Brother Hagin's fault; it's the father's fault. When he's weak scripturally and spiritually, he doesn't know his rights in Christ Jesus.

Because the husband's name is on the deed, no devil or any kind of foul spirit has the right to operate or even to come on that man's property because he's the head of the house. No demon has any right to attack his wife and children. The husband has to know that. If he doesn't know his rights, those devils can walk straight into his living room and try to put a disease on some member of his family.

I should never have let the devil put those growths on my daughter's body in the first place; and once they were there, I didn't know what to do. God doesn't bless ignorance, but He always blesses His Word. You can depend on that forever!

As soon as the Lord finished talking to me, my normal senses began to return. I was standing again in my own living room. This wasn't something I just dreamed up; it took me about five minutes to get back into the natural. God restored my natural senses by degrees.

The moment I had completely returned to the natural realm, the devil said "Don't go to see your daughter right now. Her boyfriend is with her and you'll embarrass her. Have mercy. Wait until tomorrow."

Whenever you hear, *"Wait!"* it's the devil. He'll do and say everything he can to keep you from doing what God wants you to do.

My Faith Confession

Jesus told me the same thing Brother Hagin had told Zona: "Curse those growths and they'll disappear." I made up my mind then to walk into the den where Zona and her boyfriend were sitting and do what I knew to do. When I made that decision, the power of God began to work in me. The gift of faith rose up inside me.

Now all of us want to be nice to everyone. I didn't want to embarrass Zona. But when power began to come up inside me, I couldn't see anything except victory. I had power in my fingers, in my feet and in my mouth!

So I walked into the den and said: "Zona, I'm not taking you to the hospital tomorrow or any other time. I just got back from heaven. I talked with Jesus. He told me that if I would curse those knots on your body (in His name) and believe Him for it, they would die and disappear."

Then I put my hands on Zona and said: "You devil, I'm the head of this house and this girl belongs to me. These knots and warts have to leave her body, in Jesus' name. I curse them to the root and command them to die. Growths, in Jesus' name, get off my daughter's body! Thank You, Lord, for removing them."

When I finished, I turned and walked away, still thanking Jesus. Before leaving the room, I said to Zona and her boyfriend, "Remain as you were."

As I was walking down the hallway, I said: "Thank You, Jesus, for removing those ugly knots and warts off my daughter's body. It's so wonderful to have a daughter with a body that's clear of all those knots and warts. She's free from them! Thank You, Lord, for removing them!"

I was talking my own faith in my own house!

I can't go to your house and claim healing for your family; I'm not the head of your house. God does in *your* home what *you* allow Him to do. If you haven't been doing much, He hasn't been doing much. The more you confess the Word, the more He will be able to manifest.

The next day I went to my office saying, "Thank You, Lord, for removing all the knots and warts from my daughter's body. Thank You for doing it, in Jesus' name."

I must have made that confession of faith thousands of times for a month. I said it as I lay in bed, as I walked through the house, as I got out of the car, as I went to lunch.

One day, I met Zona in the hallway. As a habit by then, I said, "Thank You, Lord, for removing all the knots and warts from my daughter's body, in Jesus' name."

She said: "Daddy, you've said that thousands of times for two weeks! I can hear you saying it when I get up in the morning and when I go to bed at night. You say it over and over, all day long. But look at me: the knots are still there! See?"

"No, I don't see anything except new hands."

"Daddy, you're driving me nuts! Can't you see them?"

"No!"

"Daddy, they're right there!"

"Where? I'm looking through the eyes of faith. I'm calling you free from all knots and warts. They can't operate in my house. I'm the head of this house, and I say they can't, in Jesus' name!"

After about thirty days of confessing this over and over again, I was on the back porch one afternoon when Zona got home from school. She came to the door and said: "Daddy, I want to ask you a question. For two or three years there have been forty-two growths on my body. I count them every day. Today there were only thirty-four. Where did eight of them go?"

"I don't know, honey, but the only choice the other thirty-four have is to go with them! I'm the head of this house, and I'm not giving them any other choice."

Then I began to thank God for what He was doing: "Thank You, Lord, that my daughter's body is free from all knots and warts!"

Sometimes I would sing as I walked back to my bedroom, "Thank You, Lord, for removing the warts and knots from my daughter's body." In the next room, I could hear Zona answer me: "Daddy, they're not going."

Sometimes I'd walk the floor, saying: "Lord, it's so wonderful to have a daughter with a body that has no knots or warts. Glory to God! They've been cursed in Jesus' name and they can't stay on her body. Knots and warts, I'm talking to you. Are you listening to me? You have to get off my daughter's body, in Jesus' name!"

I could hear Zona saying, "My daddy is flipping out!" Zona is bold in her speech, so she says whatever comes to her. She gave me a hard time, but I acted as though she hadn't said a thing and I just kept on confessing.

Healing Is Manifested!

About a week later, I was in the kitchen not thinking about anything special, when suddenly I heard a loud crash from Zona's room. She came running down the hall, yelling: "Daddy, look at me! I've got new hands and new legs! I was hanging my dresses in the closet, and my hands were as horrible-looking as they've been for three years. But when I reached down to pick up another dress, I had new hands!"

She was holding up her hands, looking at them. God had removed every blemish! The skin on her legs, knees, hands and arms was shining. It was rosy-looking, like a baby's skin.

"Daddy, I know you love the Lord; I love Jesus too. But my faith wasn't as great as yours. I've spent lots of nights in my room, weeping and begging Jesus to give me new skin. I wanted new hands more than anything else in the world. I can understand God doing something for you because you work for Him. But just think, Jesus loves a high school girl like me enough to give me new hands!"

When I took her hands and looked at them, the glory of the Lord rolled in. We stood there together, weeping.

Zona now says to me: "When you tell about my healing, be sure to say that after the doctor removed the growths, they came back along with their cousins; but when Jesus removed them, they *never* came back!"

Zona went from having the ugliest hands in her school to having the prettiest! Thank You, Jesus!

Throw the Devil Off Your Property

If the devil gets in your house, use the doctrine of the Church—the laying on of hands.

Suppose you pray like this: "Lord, one of my kids was sick last month and now the other one is sick. We're a Christian family, so I don't know why this had to happen to us. The devil just won't leave us alone." Praying like that makes you sound as crazy and ignorant as the devil!

You should shut your mouth, be bold enough to lay your hands on your children and say, "No, you don't, you dumb devils! In Jesus' name, get off my children's bodies and get out of this house!" Then begin to praise the Lord because your children are healed. When you do that, disease symptoms will have to disappear.

If your child is worse the next day, lay hands on him again and repeat what you said the day before. If he gets worse the day after that, then do it again. Keep doing it until the results come. As the days go by, you have to get stronger, not weaker.

The devil will say, "I ought to wreck the whole family and make everybody sick, but I can't keep this affliction here; the head of this house won't let me." When you show the devil that you don't have any quitting sense, he will leave.

If you're the head of the house, you need to be strong, especially if your house is full of kids.

In the late '60s, John Osteen was one of the field evangelists in greatest demand in Charismatic circles. One Sunday night when he spoke at our church in Tennessee, everyone got baptized in the Holy Ghost. People had flooded the front of that church and they all were talking in tongues. Our pastor said, "That's the first time I've ever seen a two-week revival in one day." God's glory had come in and saturated the place!

After a meeting like that, John would call home and find out that one of his children was sick. He would have another tremendous meeting, full of miracles and healings, then call home later to find that another child was sick. Sometimes even John's wife, Dodie, would be sick.

He said: "This is crazy! I hold a meeting and God heals people everywhere, then I go to my hotel room and call home only to find that something is wrong with one of the kids. Sometimes I don't even want to call home."

One day he was in their living room about to leave for a meeting when Dodie said, "John, you had better not go. Some of the children are feeling bad. One is already sick."

He finally got tired of everybody being sick, so he said, "Devil, you're not going to make my family sick!" He got all five of his kids together and said, "Come on, kids, we're going to make a choo-choo train." He had them form a line behind him, each one putting his hands on the waist of the one in front of him.

Together they marched around the house, yelling, "Devil, you're a liar! You're not going to make this family sick!" Then they marched around confessing: "God has healing power! No devil can make us sick! No devil can set foot on our property! The blood of Jesus keeps us whole!" Like a choo-choo train, they said over and over, "I put the blood over us! I put the blood! I put the blood!"

You may say, "Brother Norvel, that's silly. I'd feel like a nut."

That doesn't matter. Go ahead and do it anyway. If you don't want to, then stay sick. Zona thought I was strange; but when I cursed those growths like Jesus told me to, she got healed! To keep the devil away from your family and off your property, you have to pay a price.

God Heals Deformed Girl

I knew a woman who confessed for fourteen years that her deformed daughter was healed. The girl wasn't deformed because of disease; she was born crippled. Her hands and feet were deformed. Her mouth was so twisted that she couldn't even eat.

Throughout those fourteen years, no one around that mother believed Jesus would do it, but He did! He made that young girl normal.

Right after the child was born, the mother had started praying: "Jesus, You said in Mark 9:23 that **all things are possible to him that believeth.** In Matthew 21:22, You said I could have anything when I pray. My daughter is included in *all things,* so I'm believing for You to come to my house and make my daughter normal."

That woman's family wasn't Full Gospel. They didn't have healing services in their church, but they did have a good salvation message. No matter what denomination you belong to, you have a right to believe the Bible—you have a right to believe that it is God's will to heal.

Sometimes people who haven't been baptized in the Holy Ghost can believe the Bible better than a Full Gospel person. All anyone has to do to believe the Bible is to make up his mind to do it. Jesus said in Matthew 21:22, **Whatsoever ye shall ask in prayer, believing, ye shall receive.** God wants you to ask in prayer because He likes for you to be reverent. Then as this verse says, when you believe, you *shall* receive—not *might* receive.

God Isn't on a Time Clock

Your faith will pay off every time. Getting a healing is simple, but you have to talk your faith until the healing manifests. You need to use the right words if you want God to work for you when you're confessing.

This woman spoke the word *normal* and talked her faith for fourteen years. Then one day, Jesus came to her house and touched the girl in the wheelchair. Ten seconds later, that girl jumped up and was completely normal!

I've told about this mother's faith for years and have appeared with the daughter on television.

I teach how your faith can get a total healing for your children until they're grown if they live on your property. I teach that you can't put God on a time clock.

For a healing to manifest, it may take years of believing .

and confessing, or it may take only five minutes. If God delays the manifestation, your emotions won't want to be glad while you're believing because you want it so bad; but once the manifestation comes, you'll see why it was delayed and be glad God delayed it.

Don't try to get your friends to believe with you; that's the worst mistake you can make. Most of them only believe certain things in the Bible and won't confess and believe with you.

If that mother had found ten people in a Full Gospel church to believe with her for her daughter's healing, three of them would have dropped off after the first six months. After a year, she probably would have lost three more. If God hadn't answered in two years, the others would have left too.

You're dealing with God, not with the people around you. When God says something to you, all He wants is for you to be intelligent enough to believe it. If you do, then God Himself will come to you.

Confessing the Word of God builds your faith so that you can believe for yourself. Confess the Bible on your own; believe it on your own.

If you're head of the house, you have to believe for yourself. You can go through your house confessing the same as I can. If God did it for me, He will do it for you. He doesn't love me more than He loves you. When you know your rights in Christ Jesus as head of your house and claim healing for your family, then thank God and praise Him His power will come into your house and heal!

Obedience Brings Healing and Deliverance

God will give you an added blessing when you have strong standards for your children. They'll be proud of you, as I was of my father.

Zona is proud of me. Sometimes she sits down beside me, lays her head on my shoulder and starts to cry, saying: "I thank the Lord all the time for giving me a daddy like you. Sometimes I pinch myself to make sure I'm your daughter. If it hadn't been for your faith, I'd be dead now."

She was referring to the time I used my faith as head of the house to bring her back to God after she had backslidden. She had gone so far away from God that she had joined a gang. Five members of her gang—young people—had died. I got half beaten down trying to stand in faith to bring her back to God.

When I was holding a meeting in Texas, the Lord manifested Himself to me and said:

"Your faith is strong for healing and in other areas, but it isn't strong enough to get your daughter back. She'd like to come back to Me, but she can't. The little bit of faith she has left in Me isn't strong enough for Me to be able to manifest Myself and come to her. It's not strong enough for her to give up the nightclubs, the new set of friends and the worldly desires she's been involved in for three years. Those spirits of darkness have grabbed her."

The Lord told me that even though my faith wasn't strong enough to get Zona to come back to Him, it was strong enough to enable Him to manifest Himself to her.

As a result, He brought her back.

When God repairs something, He makes it better than it was before. Since God brought Zona back out of sin into His family, she loves me now about three times as much as before I stood in the gap for her.

As head of my house, I was willing to obey God when He told me to confess for Zona's healing and later for her deliverance. She was healed and delivered through my faith as the head of the house.

8

Jesus Heals Through the Gifts of Healing

Now concerning spiritual gifts, brethren, I would not have you ignorant.

1 Corinthians 12:1

God doesn't want you to be ignorant of His healing power. Healing is a gift to the Church. It's only one gift, but it's called *gifts,* because the name applies to more than one kind of healing. God's Word says:

... to another [is given] the gifts of healing by the same Spirit.

Corinthians 12:9

There are all kinds of healing gifts to heal all kinds of needs. For instance, God has one gift of healing that will lift a person out of a wheelchair. When I'm teaching on the gifts of healing, God's healing power will many times start to come on someone in the congregation. If that person will yield himself to God's power, he will be healed.

One time I was teaching this message to a congregation of about 1,500 people at a Bible school in Florida. I saw a woman in a wheelchair, so I had her pushed down front so she could hear me better.

About halfway through my sermon, I looked down and saw the healing power of God all over her. She'd been crippled for years; but when that power suddenly came on her, she began to shake. After about five minutes, she stood up! God just shook her as she stood there, then she sat back down again. The lady who brought her to church told how that woman had never been able to stand before.

As I kept on with my teaching, God would shake her and she'd stand up. She did that five or six times. God must have shaken her for at least thirty minutes. At last, she took a step, then two. The last time I saw her, she was walking out the door of that church! God's power can even get in a wheelchair with you!

Any time the warm healing power of God begins to come on you, you need to put some action to your faith and yield yourself to it. His healing power is available to you!

God has a gift of healing for cancer, another one for flu, another one for pain. He doesn't want anyone to be ignorant of His different gifts of healing.

Attend a Church That Believes the Bible

Unless you have a good reason not to, you should go to a church that teaches about the gifts of healing. You ought to belong to a church to have fellowship. If you go to a church that doesn't teach according to the Bible, you can't listen very closely to what you hear.

You may say, "How can I believe in Acts 2:4 that says, **They were all filled with the Holy Ghost, and began to speak with other tongues, as the Spirit gave them utterance,** if the rest of the people in my church don't believe *it?*"

What the people in your church believe doesn't matter.

If you want God to help you, you have to reach the place in your life where what the whole world believes doesn't make any difference. You need to base your believing on chapter and verse in the Bible, not on a church service. God wants you to bypass man and believe Him. When what you believe is all that really matters, God will come to you.

As to whether you should stay in a church that doesn't teach according to the Bible, you need to make a choice. Do you have good reasons for staying in that kind of church?

Sometimes God will send you to a particular church as a missionary. There are many churches in America that need missionaries. You can talk to people in some churches and they'll say, "I've never seen anything like this before."

You need to show them that the only thing that matters is what the Bible says, not the ideas they've grown up believing.

When asked what your reasons are for going to your church, you may say, "Nice people go to my church," or "My family has gone there a long time; my grandfather even built the church building," or "I have so many friends there." But these aren't good reasons!

You may think your church is a nice place to go, but it might not be such a nice place if it doesn't show you how to get what you need from God. You had better check to see what you need from God and what the people in your church believe. I helped to build my church, but that didn't help me to believe the Bible.

You might think, *I don't want to change churches.* You need to reason things God's way. Did He tell you to go to that church? I know you love your pastor, but you should listen to him only if he's preaching God's Word. You have a right to listen to God's Word.

It really makes no difference what denomination you belong to. The important thing is that your church teaches according to the Bible. Learn all you can about God. Take your children to a church that isn't ashamed to teach that God will do anything for you.

God set five offices in the church: apostle, prophet, evangelist, pastor and teacher. (Ephesians 4:11) You should go to a church where people who hold these offices are allowed to come in and share from time to time with your congregation. A missionary (apostle) should come and encourage the people to never lose the vision of winning lost souls. An evangelist or prophet who operates in the gifts of the Spirit should come and minister to the people. A pastor from another church should come in and hold a revival. About once a month, a Bible teacher should hold a teaching session. The pastor should demand that members of his congregation be there at those meetings, especially those who have sick or lost children.

You can never learn more about what God's Word actually says than from a person who's anointed by God to teach. Every church needs to receive ministry from all five offices.

A cold church is dangerous because God didn't build it. A cold church that doesn't teach the Word of God, that doesn't teach salvation and that it is God's will to heal, can damn your soul *and* your body. You need to go where God boldly heals people. You can't afford to raise your family in a place where God doesn't work. It's easy to get God's healing power working in your body when you have the right teaching.

For the gifts of the Spirit to manifest through the pastor, he must have respect for chapter 12 of First Corinthians, and then teach it to his congregation. If you waste your time in a church that's ashamed to have healing services, sooner or later you'll suffer. That kind of church is out of God's will. If you fool around with people who know only a little bit about God, the devil will come in and you won't be strong enough to throw him out.

All Nine Gifts Are Important

Some ministers think that the gift of faith means having a great deal of faith, but that's not what it means. The gift of faith gives you supernatural power to do something in the natural that you couldn't do before.

Most churches are so ignorant of the things of the Bible that 50 out of 100 ministers might not be able to name the nine gifts of the Spirit, which God has freely given to the Church. They might think that love is a gift of the Spirit, but it isn't; it's a fruit of the Spirit. Lots of ministers wouldn't know that these two aren't the same.

Probably 47 out of the remaining 50 wouldn't be able to name and define all nine gifts of the Spirit, much less explain how they operate. That leaves only about 3 ministers who really know this subject.

All of the gifts of the Holy Ghost must be in operation in your church or you won't have much of a New Testament church.

If the gifts of tongues and interpretation are operating in a church, many of its members will think they have all the gifts operating. But that's only two of them. What about the other seven? All nine gifts are perfect—each is as important as the others. When you have a need, a gift of the Spirit will manifest and help meet that need.

You need to use the gifts in order for them to have full manifestation.

Years ago when God first gave the gift of healing to Kenneth Hagin, he didn't do much with it. Then while he was in New York, he got sick and the Lord said to him:

"I brought you before My throne over twenty years ago to put My fingers in the palms of your hands. I've told you over a thousand times to use the gift I gave you then, but you have never done what I wanted you to do with the healing ministry. You kept on teaching and you prayed for the sick occasionally, maybe one night a week."

"Put your own hands on your own body now, and you will be healed. Then go back to Tulsa and hold a meeting. I'm going to put My healing power in your hands stronger. Even though I put it in your hands years ago, it didn't manifest itself strongly because you never did anything with it."

God desires that all nine gifts of the Spirit come into manifestation in the Church.

> **Wherefore I give you to understand, that no man speaking by the Spirit of God calleth Jesus accursed: and that no man can say that Jesus is the Lord, but by the Holy Ghost.**
>
> **Now there are diversities [differences] of gifts, but the same Spirit.**
>
> **And there are differences of administrations, but the same Lord.**
>
> **And there are diversities of operations, but it is the same God which worketh all in all.**
>
> **But the manifestation of the Spirit is given to every man to profit withal.**
>
> **For to one is given by the Spirit the word of wisdom; to another the word of knowledge by the same Spirit;**

To another faith by the same Spirit; to another the gifts of healing by the same Spirit;

To another the working of miracles; to another prophecy; to another discerning of spirits; to another divers kinds of tongues; to another the interpretation of tongues:

But all these worketh that one and the selfsame Spirit, dividing to every man severally as he will.

For as the body is one, and hath many members, and all the members of that one body, being many, are one body: so also is Christ.

1 Corinthians 12:3-12

The manifestation of the Spirit is given to *every man.* You belong to the Body.

But now hath God set the members every one of them in the body, as it hath pleased him.

And if they were all one member, where were the body?

But now are they many members, yet but one body.

And the eye cannot say unto the hand, I have no need of thee: nor again the head to the feet, I have no need of you.

1 Corinthians 12:18-21

The nine gifts of the Spirit are: gift of faith, word of wisdom, discerning of spirits, word of knowledge, working of miracles, gifts of healing, gift of prophecy, gift of tongues and interpretation of tongues.

You may ask, "What good are the gifts of the Spirit? For instance, what good is the word of wisdom?" The word of wisdom is God speaking in you to let you know what's going to happen in the future.

"Why are the gifts of the Spirit so important?" Because not understanding how the gifts operate is dangerous. The gift of faith, the working of miracles and the gifts of healing are power gifts. Failure to recognize and operate in one gift of the Spirit could cost a person his life.

The gifts of the Spirit can only operate in people's lives as they allow them to. If your spirit is not in tune with the Holy Ghost or if you're ignorant of the fact that God is trying to show you something, you won't realize the many things that the Holy Spirit is trying to get over to you.

The gifts of the Spirit operate in you for yourself and for others around you.

As the Spirit Wills

The gifts of healing can operate in different ways. When a pastor ministers to the sick, he's obeying the Scripture: **They shall lay hands on the sick, and they shall recover** (Mark 16:18). But if he and his congregation will believe together that God will work the gifts of healing, it will come as the Spirit wills—quick like the wind.

The gifts of healing is not automatic; it doesn't come every day. In Full Gospel churches, people expect to get ten of their sick relatives healed the first night. But most of the time something like this won't happen.

The Holy Spirit wills to come and heal you if you trust God. Even though you can't tell when the gifts of healing is going to come, once it does come, it will absolutely set you free, as it did that woman in the wheelchair during our Florida meeting.

When it manifests, the minister doesn't have to pray for anyone. Crossed eyes are straightened, tongues are loosed, and deaf ears are opened. You can't *make* the gifts of the Spirit operate; they just operate. When all nine gifts began to operate through me several years ago, it just happened.

You may say, "If the gifts only operate as the Spirit wills, how do you get them to manifest in churches where they weren't operating before?"

If you teach about them, claim them and believe in them, they will come supernaturally.

Give God Freedom

You have to give God freedom. You can't *make* God do anything. If you try to make Him operate according to the way you've set up your church services, He won't. But if you give Him complete freedom and pray, He will set you free and perform miracles.

One time, a crippled girl about fourteen years old was sitting in the back of the church where I was speaking. Suddenly, while I was teaching from the Bible, she stood up! The congregation was shocked! In the middle of their uproar over the healing, I had her walk to the front. I said, "Honey, what happened to you?"

She said: "While I was sitting in the back, my legs began to get warm, and then they got hot. I felt strength coming into my crooked, twisted legs! When I made an effort to sit up, I just stood up!"

Her teenaged brother had come with her. While he was looking at his sister's knees and legs, he began walking from the back of that large church, saying, "This is my crippled sister. I helped her get out of the car, and I helped carry her inside." He kept repeating that as he stared at her legs.

This is an example of the gifts of healing in operation.

God healed that girl on His own as she sat in the back of that congregation. This kind of supernatural manifestation won't happen in a church that doesn't teach, preach and believe in the gifts of healing.

God Performs Surgery

Because I give the Holy Spirit total freedom in my meetings, He performs great miracles. Occasionally He will say to me, "I want to perform surgery." This happens sometimes once every two years, sometimes once or twice in a year.

When it happens, I can't let anyone play the piano, sing, talk or move around. If any of that starts, God stops moving. Once everything gets quiet, I call out a certain person and say to the congregation, "Watch the Holy Ghost operate." Usually when I lay hands on that person, he falls back under the power of the Holy Ghost. Then he just lies on the floor while the Holy Ghost performs surgery on him. Sometimes God's Spirit will operate for two hours.

If something needs to be removed from your body, God will remove it. If you need a part of your body replaced, He will replace it. If you have two missing ribs, He will put them in. I didn't know this kind of power was available for the Church until the first time God performed surgery in one of my meetings.

God's Power for Miracles and Healing

Let me give you an example of the way the gifts of healing and miracles operate as the Spirit wills.

There was a little 81-year-old woman who lived close to our church in Cleveland, Tennessee. Because she had solid white hair, everybody called her "Sister White." She was a holy, clean-living woman who loved the Lord. Her great faith in God was known by many.

The townspeople tell stories about what God did for her during all the years that she served Him. They tell of the time a cyclone destroyed nearly all the houses in town. When people saw that cyclone coming, they ran to their basements—everyone except Sister White. At times like that, the Spirit of God came on her. She stood in front of her picture window and said, "The cyclone won't blow my house away! I belong to God, this house belongs to God and God is bigger than a cyclone!"

That cyclone destroyed the houses on both sides of her, but it didn't harm hers!

Then there was the time that the Holy Spirit performed surgery on Sister White. She had a big knot on her jaw that had been there for quite a while. Then one day when she came to church, that knot was gone! There was no scar or sign of surgery on her face. She stood in front of the congregation and said, "The Holy Ghost operated on me this morning!"

As she told her story, the Spirit of God filled the sanctuary, and everybody sitting there just wept. She said:

"This morning I was walking through my house when the Holy Ghost said to me, 'I want to operate on you.' The presence of God suddenly filled the whole house. The Holy Ghost said, 'Get a towel from the bathroom, come back to this room and sit down in the green chair.' When I'd done that, He said, 'Spread the towel across your lap.' So I did. Then He said, 'Turn your head sideways.' When I turned my head sideways, the knot on my face suddenly fell off onto the towel!"

Sister White loved God. Because she gave Him freedom to work in her life, the miraculous healing power of God was manifested!

God Removes Diseases

I give the Holy Ghost complete freedom in my meetings. At times, He has told me to speak to diseases and tell them to disappear. After I tell diseases to die in Jesus' name, whatever is wrong with people just disappears.

Church people, including theologians, don't understand what I'm talking about when I say, "We obey God; He doesn't obey us."

If one of them says, "Let me tell you how we do it," I say, "I don't want to hear it unless you have chapter and verse to back up what you're saying." I tell them that if they go on talking, I'll hold my hands over my ears. If beliefs aren't based on chapter and verse, they aren't based on truth and they won't work.

Neutral Buildings Allow More Freedom

Many times God will perform more in a neutral building than He will in a church. Why? Because in a neutral building, you're on 50/50 territory with the devil.

People who hold grudges against other people, who don't like their pastor or who don't like other things about their church cause a certain spirit to prevail within that church. Unless people spend time loving each other and worshiping God, the Holy Ghost won't have freedom. He won't be able to rule and reign as He should.

Because the Holy Ghost loves you so much, He still blesses whenever He can. But He can't do very much in a church that's so far in the natural realm that it's out of the divine will of God. God will give just a few blessings. When the pastor lays hands on sick people, the Holy Ghost will heal only a few of them.

In an auditorium like a hotel ballroom, God can usually

do five times as much as He will in some churches, even Full Gospel churches. I can walk in with my own faith in God's Word and bind the devil in Jesus' name. God's healing power will flow freely when you let it.

One time in an auditorium meeting as I was walking to the platform with Charles and Frances Hunter, two cripples got out of their wheelchairs and walked. That's the way it ought to be!

During another meeting for young people at a neutral building in Chattanooga, Tennessee, Lester Sumrall and I let God operate freely, and He performed many miracles.

It was in that meeting that we cast the devil out of a hippie leader of a Nashville cult. He had been on his way to get a load of LSD in Florida, but his car broke down outside the place where we were holding our meeting. He walked in the door and up the aisle. He had a beard, his hair was hanging down his back and an Indian headband was stretched around his head. He was wearing a sleeveless shirt, blue jeans and Indian moccasins. Under each arm he had tied a black bag and was swinging another one. Around his neck was hanging a tooth or some such weird thing.

Brother Sumrall and I had just finished speaking when this hippie walked up and said, "Something is playing tricks on my mind. Something told me to come up here."

We told him that "something" was the Holy Ghost. We took his hands and started praying for him. We took authority over that devil in Jesus' name and commanded it to turn him loose. We yelled, "Come out of him!" At that moment, God's power hit him. He just broke down and began to weep.

God moved strong during that meeting. Brother Sumrall had to leave town but before he left, he said, "Norvel, you ought to keep this meeting going; God is working so freely." So

I decided to go on for a few more nights.

The Hippie's Story Was Told

A few nights later, several television people came to the meeting. They had seen that hippie on different programs, telling how he had been in the penitentiary three times. He told about how before he came to Chattanooga, he was a bank robber who knew nothing about God. Then he shared the story of how he was set free. He said: "When those men cast the devil out of me, I fell in love with Jesus. I hadn't even known God was real, but I found out that Jesus loves me!"

A man as weird-looking as he was, witnessing about Jesus on television, got the attention of those television people. The Chattanooga paper ran some half-page spreads about him. He was popular around there for a while.

When those television people came to my meeting, one of them said: "We've read in the Bible about casting out devils, but before we heard that hippie we didn't know anybody did such things today. We've come here to see what's going on." [Before that service, some of us had prayed for two hours claiming that God's power would come in and heal the people. We gave God freedom to heal.]

I said: "God's power isn't a secret. Sit down and I'll tell you what's going to happen. We're going to sing a few choruses of praise to God and worship Him for a few minutes. Then two or three young people who were saved or healed will give their testimonies. After that one of these young boys will preach; then I'll speak."

"While this is happening, God will come in. One touch from Him will set people free. Jesus can touch cancer, and it will leave immediately. The divine healing power of God can flow down from heaven through mortal bodies to put every part of them back in shape again. Not only that, but it will drive out every symptom of disease and strengthen every bone in those bodies. God's divine healing power will do it. But people have to know that it's available to them. Most people believe Jesus loves them, but they aren't sure what He will do for them.

"You need to believe Him and turn Him loose in your own spirit. He will do anything you let Him do. Jesus does good things for you because He loves you. You need to get the Word of God inside you. Until you do, you'll have your own version of Jesus, and your version won't work. It has to be the same as God's version. By finding God's version in the Scriptures, you'll find out that He can set you free."

God's Healing Power Came in That Place

That night as we were speaking, the glory of God's divine healing power began to come in through the wall to my right. It passed over the congregation and went out through the wall to my left. As it moved slowly over the congregation—lasting about two minutes—people received everything they wanted from God.

One boy whose eyes had been crossed all his life couldn't see anything without thick glasses. When God's divine healing power passed over that congregation, his eyes straightened and he received 20/20 vision. He cried out, "I can see without my glasses!" The people who knew him said that with his eyes straight he didn't even look like the same person.

If you give God's healing power freedom, it will come into manifestation. When it passes over and through people as it did in that meeting, it's so holy, so clean and pure, so powerful that it drives out every symptom of disease. That's what

God's power is for: to demolish diseases. It gets rid of cancer, blindness—everything!

Because we were in a neutral building talking and preaching about divine healing power, God had freedom to perform all kinds of supernatural acts for people. He should be given the same freedom to move in every church. I'm convinced that if people would love each other and worship God more in church, most healing lines would be eliminated. God would have so much freedom. His holy Presence would so saturate the place that people would get healed before the healing line was ever formed.

To get the gifts operating in your own life, since you're a Bible believer, act like it. The Bible says to seek God for the gifts of the Spirit. (1 Corinthians 14:1) Tell God you want the gifts!

A Specific Gift of Healing

Occasionally God gives a certain gift of His healing power to a minister.

> **For to one is given by the Spirit the word of wisdom; to another the word of knowledge by the same Spirit; To another faith by the same Spirit; to another the gifts of healing by the same Spirit.**
>
> **1 Corinthians 12:8, 9**

I know of one minister who has the gift of healing for teeth. God fills teeth for nearly everyone he prays for. He has such a strong gift from God that sometimes you can look into a person's mouth and watch as teeth are being filled.

Another man prays for bad backs, and nearly everybody he prays for gets healed.

God doesn't give these special gifts to everybody. He

manifests His healing power in many different ways. After I had worked several years for God, He put His healing power into my hands as a gift. When I pray, I can feel it coming strong.

Sometimes the gifts of healing will operate along with another gift. The gifts of healing and the gift of the working of miracles are like twins. Many times, God performs a miracle and a healing at the same time.

As we saw before, all nine gifts of the Spirit are perfect. If you believe, you can always count on a gift to manifest when you need it because the gifts are perfect.

Through whatever way you receive God's healing power, once it goes through your body, it will work because it's perfect. God's healing substance comes into your body to combat diseases and demolish them. When you put your faith to work, that precious power will keep on working until it drives out of you everything that isn't supposed to be there.

9

Jesus Heals Through Anointing With Oil

Is any sick among you? let him call for the elders of the church; and let them pray over him, anointing him with oil in the name of the Lord:

And the prayer of faith shall save the sick, and the Lord shall raise him up; and if he have committed sins, they shall be forgiven him.

James 5:14, 15

God is asking the whole human race this question: **Is any sick among you?** (v. 14). God didn't leave you out. He didn't leave out your sick relatives or friends. In this verse, He asks, **Is *any* sick among you?**

Then God gives some instructions to the sick person. He says, **Let him** [the sick person, not someone else] **call for the elders of the church** (v. 14).

You may say, "Brother Norvel, I have a sick friend, so I believe that if you'll come and pray, God will heal him." But I say, "Let your friend call." You have to follow God's instructions exactly.

Verse 14 continues: **...let them [the elders] pray over him,**

anointing him with oil in the name of the Lord. Nearly every church believes in praying in the name of the Lord, but some don't believe in using oil.

If your church doesn't believe in using oil, then go to one that does. This verse can't work for them if they don't have oil. When Scripture says to use oil, it means exactly that: *Use oil!*

Learn the Word

No matter what method God uses to heal, certain things have to be done in order to receive healing.

Before you can be healed according to James 5:14, 15, you first have to be aware that the Word teaches this method of healing. You have to learn what the Bible says.

God's instructions are in the Bible. You don't believe the Bible until you obey it. You can play games with people, but you can't play games with God. God doesn't play games. If you don't have God's Word as the foundation for your believing, if you don't believe the Scriptures and quote them, then you don't really have anything. The kind of church building or the number of programs you have doesn't really matter. God isn't interested in church programs; He's interested in chapter and verse coming out your mouth.

God will be satisfied with your believing only when you make certain Scriptures a part of you, just as your right arm is a part of you.

Many people think they believe the Bible, but they don't really. Just saying you believe it is no sign that you do; you have to *show* God that you do. You obey God; He doesn't obey you. You can't go to a Gospel service and expect God to give you everything you want regardless of what you do. He requires certain things from you. You have to be willing to do what He wants you to do. In order to find out what He wants you to do, you have to learn His Word—chapter and verse.

You don't have to take a complete course at a Bible school to learn how to be healed. God's Word is so powerful that just one verse of Scripture will heal you—if you receive it.

One Verse Away From Healing

You can change things today to get your healing. Even if you're crippled, you can become normal. You're only one verse away from healing.

You can't read the Bible and say, "That's true," then forget about what you just read. You have to begin to quote Scripture, and it has to become a part of you. You need to take the time to study some healing Scriptures in the New Testament. Memorize them until they get down inside your spirit.

Every person who has died before his time was only one verse away from complete healing. Most of those people probably had a Bible laying right by their bed. Many of them spent thousands of dollars trying to get well. The ones who knew about the Gospel had as many Christians praying for them as they could notify.

You may say, "I knew a good Christian lady who loved God and had people praying for her, but she died." You're trying to argue with God. That lady was one verse away from healing. It's good to pray, but God doesn't promise healing just through prayer.

Your faith—faith in God's Word—is the substance.

Some people have strong faith, but they don't really know what they have faith in. They just have faith. That isn't good enough. Just having faith in Jesus or faith that God is God and that He can do anything isn't good enough either. This general kind of faith has some value, but you have to *show* God that you believe He can do anything.

The way to show God is to prove to Him that you have respect for His Word and that your faith is based on His Word. You must have faith in God's Word. You may believe God and love Him, but that kind of faith may not be good enough. If you're facing a crisis and need a manifestation from God, you have to dig in His Word to find the right Scripture and then stand on it without wavering. You have to stand boldly, without feelings, claiming the promise as yours because it's in the Bible.

God wants you to have faith in His Word. That's why He says, **Put me in remembrance** (Isaiah 43:26). God wants you to quote Scripture. He wants you to tell Him what Scripture you're believing so that your faith will be based on the Word. That will allow God to perform it and give you what you're asking. Remind God of the chapter and verse you're basing your faith on.

It doesn't do any good for you to say, "I don't know whether God promises what I'm believing for; I'm just believing." That kind of general praying won't get results. You have to know chapter and verse. To receive the manifestation, you have to zero in on God's Word and what He has actually promised.

Find the Scripture verse that covers what you want from God and boldly take it. Memorize it, get it into your spirit, then stand on it. Until you do that, your mouth won't quote it, because the Bible says, **Of the abundance of the heart his mouth speaketh** (Luke 6:45). Scripture goes from your heart to your mouth, and then out your mouth to do the work it promised to do. It heals, brings finances or does whatever it said it would do.

One girl that I knew came from an internationally known family. She was Full Gospel, but she died with cancer. She'd been prayed for by thousands of Full Gospel, Spirit-filled, tongue-talking Christians. Jesus told me to try to get her to believe one verse of Scripture, so I went to her house. I said to her, "God told me to come and give you this verse of Scripture so that you could live and not die. If you'll believe it, that disease will disappear."

When I reached out to pray for her, she began to weep. She wanted to believe but couldn't. Then her mother said, "Brother Hayes, our daughter has been taught divine healing all her life."

Maybe the minister of a Full Gospel church prays for the sick and its members believe in divine healing, but that's no sign you'll receive healing there. If a thousand New Testament evangelists prayed for you, but you didn't believe the Scriptures, you wouldn't get healed. It makes no difference what other people believe; it's what *you* believe that counts with God.

When your spirit has been reborn by God, the Greater One comes to live inside you. Luke 17:21 says the kingdom of heaven is within you. In other words, the Holy Ghost Who lives in your innermost being (John 7:38), can get you anything that heaven offers you now. The Holy Spirit in you thinks exactly like God thinks. He's a divine Person Who has come to live in you and give you instructions about heaven. Chapters 21 and 22 of Revelation describe all the good things in heaven.

The Holy Spirit tries to get over to you the things you need but if you don't read the Bible, you'll be so caught up in the natural realm that you can't listen to Him. He can't get over to you the Scripture you need because it isn't in your spirit. **So then faith cometh by hearing, and hearing by the word of God** (Romans 10:17). When you get the Scriptures inside you, faith will rise up in you for the particular need you have.

When you have a need, memorize the verse of Scripture that covers that need. Quote that Scripture verse over and over—two or three thousand times, if necessary. After you've done that, the Scripture will be inside you. The next time the devil comes and tries to put something on you, that Scripture will come alive inside you. Then the Holy Spirit will take that Scripture into the natural part of you.

The more Word you've learned, the easier it will be for you to fight the devil. When he comes to you, you can say to him like Jesus did, "It is written," and then quote the Scriptures.

Fight the Devil Like Jesus Did

One day as I was driving down the road, the Spirit of the Lord said to me, "I want you to start teaching My Church to fight the devil the same way I did."

One way Jesus fought the devil was by casting out demons. The other way is described in the third and fourth chapters of Matthew. After Jesus was baptized by John in the Jordan River, He was led by the Spirit into the mountains where He fasted for forty days and forty nights. During that time, the devil manifested and brought temptations to Him. But each time the devil spoke to Him, Jesus said, **It is written...**

If God heals you and the symptoms come back, the devil will try to talk you out of your healing. Every time he tries that, just say to him, "It is written," then quote chapter and verse, usually the one verse you're believing. You'll whip him every time!

When the Spirit spoke to me in the car that day, He was telling me to read the Bible to the devil. Satan can't overpower God's Word. He won't give up easily, but he *will* give up eventually. He gets tired of listening to the Bible, especially when he realizes you aren't going to give up.

Obey Without Questioning

You have to show God that you trust what He says exactly. If you question or analyze or doubt the Bible, you aren't acting as though you trust God. Watch your mouth. Saying one time the words, *But, Jesus...*, will keep the power of God's Word from working for you.

The hardest thing for some Christians to do is read a verse in the Bible, believe it and then do it. Christians have to quit talking and show God some action. When they do, God's power will give them the help or freedom they need.

Matthew 14:14-21 describes the miracle of multiplication with five loaves and two fishes. Jesus had spoken to a multitude of five thousand men, plus women and children, and healed their sick.

The disciples said to Jesus, "We ought to send these people to the villages to buy food."

Then He said, "You give them something to eat."

"But, Jesus, we only have two fishes and five loaves of bread."

Jesus had said to them, "You give them something to eat," not "I will give them something to eat." But then the disciples began to question Him and analyze things.

When they started saying, "But, Jesus...," He said, "Bring the loaves and fishes to Me." He looked up to heaven, asked God to bless the food and prayed, "Thank You, Father, for feeding these people." Then He broke the bread. He had to break all of it Himself; nobody else had enough faith to break it. He gave the food to the disciples, and the disciples passed it out to all the people.

Jesus was God manifested in the flesh. If the disciples had obeyed without question, they could have done what Jesus did: they could have broken the bread, passed it out and fed the entire multitude themselves.

God honors the kind of faith it takes to obey without questioning. There are several examples of this in the Bible, including the Old Testament. We're living under a new covenant that puts us in a better position for God to honor this kind of faith and give us what we need. You have to learn to obey immediately. If you do, it will change your life.

The Bible is already written and established in heaven. Make up your mind that you can receive great manifestations from God just from one verse of Scripture. When you do, God's power will give you what that verse says.

God Performs His Word

When you've learned what the Bible says to do and then have done it, God will perform His Word.

According to Jeremiah 1:12, God Himself looks over His Word twenty-four hours a day—with a sharp eagle eye— to perform it. He performs His Word, not *your* version of it. You have to do exactly as God's Word says.

If you stop quoting Scripture, God stops working. God's Word has already been spoken and written. What it says will automatically be done if you let it. God will perform any verse of Scripture for any person who will obey.

When disease comes and tries to fasten itself onto you, those Bible verses you've memorized, those words inside you, have already come out the mouth of God. When those same verses come out your mouth, it will bring power and victory to you.

All you have to do is hunt Scripture and stand on it. It'll bring you up from a death bed. Let me say it again: You're only one verse away from healing. But you have to take hold of the Scriptures and not let go. Any verse of Scripture that promises you something in the New Testament will bring God's power to you. But you have to know that; you have to make that verse of Scripture a part of you.

A few years ago, God gave me a new method of teaching to encourage people to obey the Scriptures. He said to me:

> *The invitations for salvation, for the baptism of the Holy Ghost and any other general invitation are good because people can receive from Me when they come and ask. But unless I direct you otherwise, I want you to stop giving those invitations at the end of every service.*
>
> *You have been trying to talk people into believing. Instead, have the people do what you teach. If you teach on one subject and then give ten unrelated invitations, the people will have forgotten what you taught them in three days. But if they obey the words you teach, they can take home what they learned.*
>
> *If you teach on prayer, have the people pray. If you teach on praying in the Spirit, have them pray in the Spirit. If you teach about the laying on of hands or another means of using faith, have them come forward and obey what you have taught.*

God's help comes to you from the Scriptures when you obey His Word. If someone else obeys verses of Scripture for you, those verses will only work in part. God can hardly wait to heal you. All you have to do is obey the Scriptures yourself.

God Will Give You Anything

When you do what God wants, He will do what you want.

The second year I taught at Southern Illinois University, I spoke in a big, modern classroom with 400 seats arranged in tiers around the stage. The first night, as I stood looking up into the crowd, I saw the psychiatrist I've already told you about. He had brought a large group of people to that meeting.

As I was teaching that night on the goodness of God, I made a bold statement. I said, "God will do anything for you if you trust *Him*."

The moment I said that, a woman sitting close to the psychiatrist jumped up, pointed to her seat and yelled, "It happened right there when you pointed your finger at me!" (I hadn't even known that she was there or that I'd pointed my finger at her.)

"What happened?" I asked.

"I had been deaf for thirty years. But when you pointed your finger at me, my ears popped open! Now I can hear everything! My husband and I came to the service with this doctor. We've never been to a service like this before. My husband can tell you I was deaf. But now I can hear everything! It all happened while I was sitting right there in that seat!"

She kept talking like that and wouldn't quit. God made a missionary out of her, working all over that town for the next two weeks!

The things I'm sharing are not hearsay. I was there when God opened that woman's ears. The God Who can do anything performs His Word.

If you'll obey the Scriptures, God will do anything the Scriptures say He will do. If you preach a good salvation message—that Jesus loves you so much He died on the cross for you—the Holy Spirit will put sinners under conviction.

They'll run to the altar to get saved, because you have preached good salvation Scriptures. If you obey God and preach healing Scriptures, God will heal people.

Some people say salvation is more important than anything else God has for you. That kind of thinking can get you mixed up. You need to be saved first, but salvation alone won't help you if you're dying of cancer. God doesn't have a one-track mind. The Scriptures say that when you get saved, or born again, God will bring everything you need for success and victory from the time you get up in the morning until the time you go to bed at night.

When you obey God, He will give you anything. He will make you healthy. He will clear your thinking. He will bring you heaven now.

James 5:14 says to use oil. For God to perform His Word, the Scripture must be obeyed exactly.

As I mentioned earlier, when my mother and brother died, we were going to a church that didn't use oil. Our church had a blackboard with a sign over it that said, PRAY FOR THE SICK. Under that sign was written my mother's name, "Zona Hayes." They prayed for her, but she died. My brother's name stayed there for over a year, and then he died.

People all over the country know of someone who died, even though others were praying. They ask me, "Why did he die?" My answer is always the same: "He died because he didn't believe the Scriptures."

I found out that blackboards don't work. God doesn't look over a blackboard to perform it; **He looks over His Word to perform it.** (Jeremiah 1:12) Just writing a name for prayer on a blackboard isn't scriptural.

God looks over elders of the church who are praying in the name of Jesus, anointing the sick with oil and praying the prayer of faith. God looks over this because it's done according to His instructions in the Bible.

Just putting a steeple on a building and giving out your version of God won't bring healing. You have to be scriptural.

Don't Depend on Feelings

In one meeting, I taught on James 5:14,15. When I'd finished, I asked the people to line up across the front so I could pray for them. I'd been teaching that they must have faith without feelings.

This idea jars the average Christian, because people like to have feelings. God gave us feelings, but sometimes we're healed without feeling a thing.

When Zona was healed—when those growths disappeared and she suddenly received new skin—there was a quick manifestation from the Lord. But Zona didn't feel anything.

When you believe for a healing, you need to have faith in God's Word and pay no attention to how you feel. Even if you don't feel it, the power of God is in your body to bring a healing.

That night in my meeting, I told the people:

The beginning of James 5:15 says, **And the prayer of faith shall save the sick.** Save is the opposite of dying. Then it says, **and the Lord shall raise him up.** Raise means getting healed.

James 5:14, 15 will work for anyone who obeys it. Let your faith be in those Scripture verses because they're being obeyed. If you respect and believe them, your healing will manifest. Put your faith only in God's Word.

"When I anoint you with oil and pray the prayer of faith over you, you have to believe that you're healed at that moment. So believe it, even though you may not have any feelings."

I anointed each person with oil and prayed in the name of Jesus. When I reached the end of the line, I went back to the first person and asked, "When I prayed for you, did you feel anything?"

"No."

"How do you know that you're healed?"

"I know because James 5:14, 15 says I am."

As I went down the line and asked everyone the same question, each one answered the same way.

Then someone said, "I know I'm healed because the Lord heals."

I said, "You don't understand the principle yet. It won't work for you. What did I teach about tonight?"

"You taught on James 5:14, 15."

"When I anointed you with oil and prayed the prayer of faith in Jesus' name, did you feel anything?"

"No."

"Then how do you know you're healed?"

"I know I'm healed because you taught that James 5:14, 15 is the reason I'm healed."

"Now you've got it!"

As I went down the rest of the line, none of them said they felt anything.

When I finished, the Lord said to me, "Walk up and down in front of the line and teach James 5:14, 15 again. They don't have it yet."

I had already taught on this for about an hour and a half, but I hammered on for another fifteen minutes. Unless you take Scripture home with you, you don't really have it. I said:

"You're healed because God has already spoken the words in James 5:14, 15. His instructions are the truth. You're healed because I've obeyed them in your behalf by anointing you with oil in Jesus' name and praying the prayer of faith for you. You're healed, not because I'm here, but because you have faith in God's words.

"The man who obeys James 5:14, 15 in your behalf doesn't have anything to do with your healing. It's the Scriptures that heal you. John 17:17 says **the Word of God is true,** and John 8:32 says **the truth shall make you free.**

"Now you have to speak your faith. The substance is what you say, but you have to put action to your faith. When you leave this building tonight, I want you to walk to your car saying, 'I'm healed because James 5:14, 15 has been ministered to me. I'm healed because God's Word says that I am. I'm healed because it's been obeyed in my behalf.'

"If you're married, don't talk much. Save whatever you need to talk about until tomorrow. Have your wife or husband help you quote what I said as you're driving home. While you're getting ready for bed, continue to quote it. When you get in bed, quote it some more.

"If your mate has to get up early and is trying to go to sleep, then put your head in your pillow as you say: 'It's written that when the elders of the Church anoint me with oil and pray the prayer of faith, God will raise me up. James 5:14, 15 has been obeyed in my behalf; therefore, I'm healed. I'm healed because God's Word says I am.'

"Then every day say, 'My body is healed according to James 5:14, 15.' Tell God, 'James 5:14, 15 is mine.' From time to time, let the devil know you accept the Scriptures. Say to him, 'Devil, James 5:14, 15 is true. Jesus is Truth, and you're a liar!'"

After the people at the altar had promised to do as I said, I dismissed the service. The next night as I was walking toward the church after parking my car, a man called out to me. I looked back to see him running toward me. He said:

"I've heard James 5:14, 15 preached for years, but I never got it until last night. I did what you told us to do. I went to my car, quoting what you said. I went home quoting it. I took off my clothes, got in bed and turned out the lights, still quoting it.

"My feet and ankles were deformed. Though I didn't walk normally, I could at least walk; but I never could run. This church knows how I was. But I went to sleep last night quoting what you said.

"This morning when I woke up, I pulled back the covers and put my feet on the floor like I always do. As I was sitting there, I looked down to see that both my feet and ankles were normal! I was healed because of James 5:14, 15!"

The Lord decided to come in with the gift of healing. Because that man had faith without feelings, he was healed.

Obedience Brought Healing

One time when I was invited to speak at a church in New York, the Lord said, "Take a bottle of oil with you." At the end of the service, so many people came forward for healing that I had to bring them on the stage. I gently anointed them with oil in Jesus' name, and the Lord healed them. Even some Catholic nuns came up and received their healing.

God moved so strong, healing so many, that finally there was no room left, even on the stage. Sometimes when a person in a healing line gets the manifestation right then, his body can't stand it and he falls under God's power. I had to wait until some of the people were able to get up off the floor to make room for more.

After the service, the pastor said, "Mr. Hayes, my wife and I have been praying for several years for God to send His power into this church."

God sent me there with a bottle of oil and James 5:14, 15. I didn't need anything else! Because those people learned God's Word and obeyed it, God performed His Word and healed them.

10

Jesus Heals Through Special Miracles

And God wrought special miracles by the hands of Paul:

So that from his body were brought unto the sick handkerchiefs or aprons, and the diseases departed from them, and the evil spirits went out of them.

Acts 19:11, 12

Healing for Those Far Away

Acts 19:11,12 is the best passage of Scripture to use when praying for friends and relatives who don't live near you.

Several years ago when I was speaking at a Full Gospel Business Men's convention in Hamilton, Ontario, a lady from Buffalo, New York, brought a handkerchief for me to pray over. It seems that her daughter-in-law, who had intended to come to the convention, had been put in the hospital a few days before the meeting. I prayed over that handkerchief and told the lady to have her daughter-in-law put it on the afflicted place.

By the time that lady reached the hospital, her daughter-in-law had already undergone a complete hysterectomy (removal of ovaries, fallopian tubes and womb). But when she placed that handkerchief on her daughter-in-law, God healed her. Today she has received new organs!

Whenever God creates new wombs, ovaries and tubes—that's a special miracle. If you went to the average church and asked the average Christian, "Do you believe Jesus makes new wombs through handkerchiefs?" that person would say, "We don't want to get our good solid church off on something so far out."

The Bible teaches that God will perform special miracles through a handkerchief or cloth laid on a sick person's body. Diseases will leave. Demons will be driven out.

God will do special miracles to give you anything you need if you'll just obey His instructions that we've read in the nineteenth chapter of Acts.

God Wants To Use You

Verse 11 says, **God wrought special miracles by the hands of Paul**. God can't use Paul's hands today, so He wants to do miracles through *your* hands.

You may say, "God has never performed miracles through my hands." But He wants to! He wants to heal and bless people through you.

You can know God, be healed by Him, and have His gifts operating through you just as well as anyone else can. You don't have to be a famous evangelist. Sister White, that 81-year-old lady I talked about before who lived by herself in a tiny house in Cleveland, Tennessee, probably knew God better than anybody I've ever met. She knew God so well because she obeyed Him. She knew Him in a completely different way than most people do, and God talked to her.

I've taken internationally known evangelists and preachers to her house. When she talked, they got blessed.

One minister, who had just returned from preaching around the world, stopped off in Cleveland, Tennessee, to see me. When I asked if he'd like to get blessed, he said, "Sure."

"Then I'll take you to meet somebody who knows God better than you. Let's go."

When I drove up in front of Sister White's tiny house, the evangelist asked, "Norvel, what are you doing?" I said, "The person who lives in this house knows God better than you. Don't judge; just be nice. You're going to be blessed."

When we walked into that house, Sister White said, "Brother Norvel, where have you been? I've been waiting to see you for so long. It's so good to have you." (Every time she saw me, she said the same thing.)

"Sister White, I've had things to do, but I brought a friend who's been preaching around the world. I wanted him to meet you and get blessed. Tell him about the Holy Ghost operating on you."

So she began her story: "Oh, yes. I had a knot on my jaw that had been there for quite a long time ...."

Each time she told about what had happened to her, the glory of the Lord came on her. As she was talking, I looked over at my minister friend, who had been out preaching around the world. He was just weeping.

I said to him, "Get on your knees and let Sister White bless you." Sobbing, he dropped to his knees, ready to be blessed.

"Sister White, I want you to put your hands on my friend

and ask Jesus to bless him." By that time, she hardly knew where she was.

She put her hands on him and just said, "Glory, Jesus. Bless, Jesus. Oh, Jesus, bless."

God's glory was rolling in that little white house. God gave that famous evangelist a bath in the Holy Ghost by using a little elderly lady to bless him. You don't have to be famous for God to use you.

Anything I do, you can do too—if you're born again. If I can believe a certain Scripture verse, you can believe it too. If I can cast the devil out of another person, you can too. If I can lay my hands on sick people, allowing God's power to heal them, you can too. God can heal through your hands too! There's nothing supernatural about me. You can do anything I can do, maybe even better.

It's not what you *can* do, but what you *do* that makes the difference. When you do what God's Word says, the blessings of God will come on you. Many people know how to do things better than I do; but if I make a stumbling effort, God will give me the blessings. A particular theologian, who knows he's smarter than I am, can't understand why God doesn't bless him the way He blesses me.

You have to seek God for different things. You have to put God first. The Bible promises that if you put the Gospel first, all other things will be added unto you. (Matthew 6:33)

Put God First

God will manifest Himself when you put Him first, when you talk about Him and sing about Him. When you say God will do something, He does it. Not only will He manifest Himself in different ways, but He will manifest Himself by giving you anything you want in line with His Word.

For as many as are led by the Spirit of God, they are the sons of God (Romans 8:14). Once you've made up your mind to obey the Holy Ghost, you will see great manifestations of healings and workings of miracles. After the people are blessed, God will bless you. Third John 2 says, **Beloved, I wish above all things that thou mayest prosper and be in health, even as thy soul prospereth.** If you make up your mind to obey the Holy Ghost, He will give you blessings as great as the blessings He has given me.

Put the Gospel first and all other things shall be added unto you.

Follow the Leading of the Holy Spirit

When I was in Alabama, the Lord showed me that you have to learn how to be led by the Spirit of God when you're ministering. You see, the Spirit of God leads people in different ways. You can't just minister one day unless God has told you to.

When I teach on having faith without depending on feelings, people are usually healed without having any feelings. In one service, God may cause people to drop to the floor and weep before the healing power begins to come on them.

When I teach the Bible, I follow the leading of the Holy Spirit. God once told me, "I want you to teach the people what I have taught you; I want you to teach them My Word." You have to teach what God has taught you. The Lord requires me to teach on healing. But I don't have to think about what I'm going to say. I never have to hunt for words because God touches me divinely and puts words inside me. I could stand before a group and teach on healing for two months because the Holy Ghost will teach through me.

When God first started teaching through me that way, I would shake my head later, saying to myself, *Was that me? I can't believe I said all those things.*

If God Can Trust You, He Will Promote You

The more God can trust you, the more He will bless you and promote you. **He that is faithful in that which is least is faithful also in much: and he that is unjust in the least is unjust also in much** (Luke 16:10).

God will trust you first with the Gospel. Then He will trust you with something besides the Gospel to see how you do. If you do a good job with a small thing, then He will trust you with something else.

If you show God that He can trust you, He will bless you more than you could have ever dreamed possible. The blessings will come to you at the most unique and unexpected times. You won't even be thinking about them, and they'll come to you. God blessed me that way by healing Zona's warts.

Always put the Gospel first, then all other things will be added unto you. When you diligently seek God and let the devil know you mean business by confessing who you are in Christ Jesus, God will reward you and give you your healing.

Let God Use Your Hands

When you put God first, He will heal through you. Look at your hands and think, *God will bring special miracles to people through my hands.* Let Him use your hands.

When I lay my hands on handkerchiefs or cloths to be

taken to the sick, I pray like this:

Father, in Jesus' name, I lay my hands on these cloths and claim that Your healing, miracle-working and delivering power goes into them to drive out evil spirits and demons.

As these cloths are put on sick bodies, all the diseases will disappear from those bodies. All evil spirits will go out of those bodies completely, in Jesus' name, and leave the people every whit whole. If there are bodies that need special miracles, the Spirit of God shall perform them.

Father, in Jesus' name, I claim that the power of God goes into these cloths and handkerchiefs to do the work You intended and promised that they would do in Acts 19:11, 12. It is done, in Jesus' name.

11

Jesus Heals Through Praying for Others

Confess your faults one to another, and pray one for another, that ye may be healed. The effectual fervent prayer of a righteous man availeth much.

James 5:16

The Word of God says that you should pray for others, because when you do, you'll be healed.

This is an area of healing I had never taught until one time when I was holding a meeting in Honolulu, Hawaii.

While still on the flight to Honolulu, the Lord began speaking to my heart about healing. He said, "I want you to teach the people in Honolulu on a subject you have never taught before." Then He showed me James 5:16. He said, "If you will have the people in your meetings who need healing to pray for another person, then they will receive their healing as they do."

When I got to Honolulu, I was scheduled to speak in a church service on Sunday night, so I spoke on healing. Then I taught from James 5:16. I told the people about the importance of "praying for one another that you may be healed," as this Scripture says.

When I'd finished teaching, I said:

"Now this is my first public invitation based on James 5:16, but God told me that He would heal people according to that verse just the same as He heals on any other verse in His Word that promises healing. So let's just take God at His Word. The Bible says God can't lie, so that means we can get healed through James 5:16: **Pray one for another, that ye may be healed.**"

There were several hundred people in the church service that night. When I gave the invitation for them to come forward for healing, a bunch of people came up. When everybody got to the front, I said:

"I want each of you to turn to another person right now and begin to pray for that person to be healed. Don't pray for yourself. This scripture verse in James doesn't say anything about praying for yourself; it says you're to pray for one another. So start praying for the person next to you, and God will heal you too!"

As those people prayed for one another, the Lord began to heal all over the place!

Then a strange thing began to happen. As people were praying for someone else to be healed, God found so much favor in it that He began to baptize them in the Holy Ghost. One seventeen year old boy, who had just gotten saved, was praying for another person to be healed. As he prayed, a language began to bubble up out of him. Before he knew what had happened, he was baptized in the Holy Ghost and speaking in tongues!

The Holy Spirit really worked that night and brought blessing to the people. It was a beautiful experience. That was my first time to give an invitation based on James 5:16, but it wasn't my last!

Pray one for another, that you may be healed.

12

Read the Bible to Satan
and Stay Healed!

One time I was invited to San Antonio, Texas, to teach in a Bible seminar on the subject of the Holy Ghost and the gifts of the Spirit. As a result of that meeting, churches all over that city opened their doors for me to come and teach the Bible to their people.

One morning, I felt led to teach on the subject of faith. At the end of the service, one girl came forward to receive the baptism in the Holy Spirit. It was a glorious experience!

When the service was over, I went to lunch with the pastor and his wife. They said to me, "We have been preaching the Gospel for over forty years. We have watched and heard how God uses you, and we have great respect for your ministry. We want you to come back to our church and teach for a few days."

So I went back to their church on Easter Sunday and started teaching the Word of God. I stayed there and taught for four nights and then went over to the other side of the city and taught for ten nights. Each morning I was scheduled to preach at a different church.

I was speaking on Monday night to an audience with a number of ministers present. These ministers came from churches across the city. I used that familiar text, Mark 11:24, which I've referred to so often in this book. In that meeting when I gave the altar call, dozens of people flooded the front of the church to seek God.

One minister sitting in the back was so touched and moved by God that he began to scream out and push his way through the congregation under supernatural power. He came and began to hug the pulpit, holding on to it as God's power melted him to the floor. He was completely overwhelmed by the mighty presence of God.

You see, when God begins to show you the lost world that's dying and going to hell, you begin to hear the screams and groans of the people in hell, and you begin to see people dying without God. It will change you. It can so shake your natural understanding that all you want to do is get on your face before God and scream out for mercy for them.

The devil is so deceiving. He will do everything within his power to get you to doubt God's Word and to doubt God's call. He will even try to convince you that heaven and hell aren't real. He wants to dampen your vision. He wants to get you to give up your efforts in trying to win the lost and to pray for the needs all around you.

That night the great outpouring of God's Spirit was so strong. Throughout that congregation, people began to put their faith implicitly in the Scriptures, as I had read from Mark 11:24. They began to act on that Word. As a result, during the altar call about one-third of the people came for prayer or for help.

The reason I'm telling about this incident is to show you that when God's power begins to fall in a place, people's faith will mount up to the point that they can believe God for anything. To see miracles take place right before their eyes strengthens their faith even more. Those who have been slow and have hesitated to believe will immediately get hungry for spiritual things and for freedom for their own spirits and bodies.

It's not necessary to have to witness such a manifestation of power as this to get an answer from God.

Regardless of where you are, even if you're all alone, you can stand on God's Word like my deformed friend did—and God will heal you. It's your faith and God's Word that heals you!

Satan Hates the Bible

You can continue enjoying freedom from the forces and power of Satan by reading God's Word to him. You see, Satan hates the Bible because it's the Truth. He can't stand the Truth!

I may seem repetitious, but it's necessary sometimes to repeat things again and again so that the message I'm sharing will sink in.

Let me warn you again that Satan will try to prevent you from reading God's Word. He wants to occupy you with all kinds of legitimate things in life so that God's Word will be crowded out. Therefore, you should constantly be reading it, standing on it and acting on it. Even read it out loud to the devil when he tries to bring doubt into your mind. It's your shield against his fiery darts. (Ephesians 6:16)

Keeping Victory Over the Devil

The power of God is released as our faith begins to build. I'll give you an example of how faith worked through a mother and daughter.

The daughter was a concert pianist who was letting her talents die and wither away, and she was miserable. She had reached a point of desperation, so she came to me for counseling. She wanted to talk to me about the needs in her life, about her talent and about the propositions that were being offered to her by the world. As I was explaining that Jesus wanted and needed her talent to work for Him also, the mighty power of God came on us. It began to surge through her, and she was set free!

Her mother was in a similar condition. She was a nervous wreck because of so many pressures. She worked as staff secretary at a large air base, and over the years her job pressures had become unbearable. She needed help, so I prayed with her too.

I took authority over the thing that was causing those bad nerves and I commanded them to leave her in Jesus' name. Jesus came to her rescue, and the mighty power of God began to surge through her body in a supernatural way. Her nervous system was healed and restored to normal. She told me that she was completely healed. She said she had been helped in some years past, but never on a permanent basis.

The reason she hadn't received permanent relief through prayer was that she didn't know how to fight against the devil and his forces. I told her that in order to keep the victory, she had to read the Bible to the devil. But she didn't understand what I meant. So I said:

"I'm going to teach you how to fight the devil. The best way I know to fight him is to follow the instructions of James. You have to rebuke the devil in the name of the Lord, and he has to flee from you. That means don't yield yourself to your own understanding, to any kind of symptoms of pain or heartache. Resist them all in the name of Jesus, and stand your ground. Jesus wants you to be free of pain. He wants you to be full of joy every day of your life."

Then she asked: "What will happen to me when I go back to the office tomorrow and all that pressure begins to fall on me as it has in times past? It's been years since I've felt like this, and I don't want to lose it. In just five minutes, the power of God has changed me from a miserable, nervous wreck to a life that's filled with peace, joy, understanding and the promise of a thrilling future."

That's when I told her what to say to the devil.

"Mr. Devil, I'm Going To Read the Bible to You"

I said to her:

"I want you to take your Bible to work and lay it on your desk. Satan will come at you tomorrow and try to take you back to the life you had yesterday. When he does, I want you to say this to him:

"'Mr. Devil, I don't know if you can read or not, but just in case you can't, I'm going to read the Bible to you. I'll show you why I'm completely healed and why I'll never be nervous again so long as I live—I'll prove to you that my life will be a life of peace, health and beauty.

"Devil, I want to read Mark 11:24 to you. Now you listen and you'll find out why I'm healed and why I'm going to remain healed.'"

I also told her to read Mark 11:23 to him. It says:

For verily I say unto you, That whosoever shall say unto this mountain, Be thou removed, and be thou cast into the sea; and shall not doubt in his heart, but shall believe that those things which he saith shall come to pass; he shall have whatsoever he saith.

That mountain could be any number of things. It might be a nervous condition, a spirit of fear, a physical handicap, a binding habit, a financial problem or an incurable disease. But that mountain is simply nothing compared to the power of Almighty God. By quoting this Scripture verse to the devil, he will have to turn loose his hold on the life of the believer.

She Reminded Satan of Her Healing

As I continued talking with that lady, I said to her, "You've received what you needed from God as you stood right here in this house. Is that right?"

"Absolutely," she said. "I'm completely healed, completely free. I haven't had joy and peace like this in years."

"Then will you do as I tell you to do?"

"Yes, I will."

"All right, you need to read the Scripture verse I've just quoted to you. Read it out loud as you're sitting there at your desk, so that Satan can hear you."

She promised to do so.

She came to church the next night and gave a public testimony, telling of the marvelous way her life had been changed. She said:

"I'm not the same woman I was two days ago. I would advise you people to listen to God's Word and do the same thing I did. I went to work today and took my Bible with me, and the pressure began to come on me as it had in times past. Because of the confusion, that nervous condition began trying to return to my body. So I picked up my Bible and said, 'Mr. Devil, I'm going to read you something.' Then I turned to Mark

11:23 and I read it.

"Then I said, 'Mr. Devil, I say that I'm healed and that I'll never be nervous again. Your tormenting days with me are over. My foundation is based on the promise of Jesus in Mark 11:24.' Then I read that Scripture verse out loud to the devil. I said, 'Now, **what things soever** means my nervous system in this case.' As I prayed with Brother Hayes, we agreed and God's power set me free. I desire to stay healed, so I will stay free. I have my healing now and forever!"

After she had taken that kind of stand against the devil orally, speaking as if she were talking to an individual, Satan fled instantly. She said that the tormenting, confusing force began to leave in a matter of seconds, and she had no more trouble.

But as a reminder to Satan, she spoke out loud again: "Now, Satan, I have received power in my body from God and by His help. You'll never rob me of that peace and power again. If you try to, I'll read my Bible to you again; and when I do, you'll have to flee. I believe what it says, and I'll stand on it now and forever!"

This family invited me to come to their home for Sunday dinner. The mother and her husband, the daughter and her husband, and other members of the family were there. It was obvious that these people's lives had been changed by the power of God. They had taken authority over the power of darkness that had been coming against their minds and bodies, and even their homes.

"It Is Written"

Not only they, but you, dear reader, have that same authority if you'll just take it now in the name of Jesus Christ.

Jesus said that Satan, **the enemy, had come to kill and steal and destroy, but that He (Jesus) had come that we might have life and have it more abundantly.** (John 10:10) We don't have to be beaten down or bullied by Satan's deceptive tactics. We can have victory through quoting God's Word to him.

It's dangerous for us to build our faith on the doctrines and philosophies of men; they are as sinking sand. But we have to be strong and build our faith on the Rock, Christ Jesus, and His entire Word.

There's no other way to resist the devil but through God's Word. Don't just ask him to leave you, your mind and your body, and those of your loved ones he's afflicting, but quote the Word of God to him and command him to go!

Before Jesus began His earthly ministry, after He had fasted forty days and nights, Satan attacked Him at His weakest moment. He tempted Jesus in every way that mankind can be tempted—on the pride of life, on the hunger of the flesh, on the lust of the eyes. But Jesus overcame the devil each and every time by quoting the Word of God to him! Each time He said, **It is written...,** referring to the Old Testament. You can read this account in Matthew 4:1-11.

This is one of the greatest secrets in God's Word, and we're to overcome the enemy the same way. It's a revelation from God's Truth that we can overcome him everywhere, every time, in every situation and every circumstance!

We not only have the promises of the Old Testament, as Jesus had, but now we have the New Testament too. It gives us even greater power and greater promises and authority through Jesus Christ, Who came to fulfill the Law of God to its very last letter.

Satan Is a Defeated Foe

Satan is still tempting and attacking, harassing and deceiving. His demon spirits are being unleashed on the human race like never before. This battle will go on until Jesus returns to earth and sends the devil off to his place of eternal punishment.

In the meantime, we as believers cannot panic or get discouraged. We have to rise up and quote God's Word to the devil. We have to stand on God's promises until the battle of all ages comes to an end.

In Revelation 12:11, the apostle John says this about the overcomers: **And they overcame him** [that old dragon, the devil] **by the blood of the Lamb** [Jesus Christ], **and by the word of their testimony.** The blood is the shield and the Word is the sword that always defeats the enemy.

Satan is a defeated foe. He was defeated at Calvary. His works were defeated. His power was defeated. His authority was defeated. It was stripped from him and given to the Church—all truly born-again believers who've accepted Jesus Christ as their Savior and are keeping His commandments.

Accept the challenge! Rise up now, believe God and praise Him out loud for the victory over all the works of the devil. It's your prerogative, your divine privilege through the power, blood and name of Jesus. Rise up and do it now. Your faith can heal you!

Conclusion

We don't have to pay for healing; it's a free gift to the Church.

To get your healing, you have to make up your mind that it's for you, then ask for it and take it. You have to pass God's test, over chapter and verse, by watching yourself and making sure the words you speak agree with God's Word. When you put the Gospel first and then confess what you want, God will give it to you. You can enjoy heaven on earth now.

To get God's healing power to work, no matter what the method, keep everything simple and give God freedom. Simple faith pleases God. **Be still, and know that I am God** (Psalm 46:10). Know that the Bible, God's Word, is exactly what John 17:17 says it is—the Truth. According to John 8:32, the Truth will set you free!

Stop wondering whether or not the Lord will heal you. The devil and human beings try to put that thought in your mind. Don't express that thought through your own words; get it out of your mind and out of your system!

If Jesus has ever healed one person, He will heal you. God's healing power is *always* available. Jesus will heal you every time!

Is Jesus *Your* Savior?

Before you pray the prayer for healing, read this:

The Bible says that **all have sinned and come short of the glory of God** (Romans 3:23). It also says that **the wages of sin is death; but the gift of God is eternal life through Jesus Christ our Lord** (Romans 6:23) and that **Christ died for our sins** (1 Corinthians 15:3).

The Bible also says, **for by grace are ye saved through faith; and that not of yourselves: it is the gift of God:** (Ephesians 2:8) and that **if thou shalt confess with thy mouth the Lord Jesus, and shalt believe in thine heart that God hath raised him from the dead, thou shalt be saved** (Romans 10:9, 10).

If you have never received Jesus as Your Savior, accept Him now! Pray this out loud:

Father, I thank You that Christ died for my sins and because of that I can have eternal life with You as a free gift by believing in Him. I confess with my mouth the Lord Jesus and believe in my heart that God raised Him from the dead. I thank You, Lord, for saving me and that I will live with you for eternity! In Jesus' name, amen.

Prayer for Healing

If you need healing, pray this prayer from your heart:

I thank You, Jesus, that because my name is written in heaven. I have a right to God's healing power. I confess with my mouth because I believe in my heart that the healing power of God Almighty is raging through my body to bring a cure to me. I believe God's power is is my body, working to give me a miracle of healing.

*Thank You, Lord, because I'm healed. I'm not **going to be** healed; I'm healed now in Jesus' name.*

Norvel Hayes shares God's Word boldly and simply with an enthusiasm that captures the heart of the hearer. He has learned through personal experience that God's Word can be effective in every area of life, and that it will work for anyone who will believe it and apply it.

Norvel owns several businesses which function successfully despite the fact that he spends more than half his time away from the office, ministering the Gospel throughout the country. His obedience to God and his willingness to share his faith have taken him to a variety of places. He ministers in churches, seminars, conventions, colleges, prisons—anywhere the Spirit of God leads.

For a complete list of tapes and books by Norvel Hayes, write:

Norvel Hayes

P. O. Box 1379

Cleveland, TN 37311

Feel free to include your prayer requests and comments when you write.

Other Books by Norvel Hayes

Divine Healing

Endued with Power

God's Light

How to Become a Wise Man in God's Eyes

How to Cast Out Devils

Know Your Enemy

Pleasing the Lord

Stand in the Gap

How to Get Your Prayers Answered

What Causes Jesus to Work Miracles

Confession Brings Possession

Faith in Action

Getting to Know God

The Blessing of Obedience

Number One Way to Fight the Devil

What to Do For Healing

God's Light

Financial Dominion

God's Power Through the Laying on of Hands

How to Get God's Attention

How to Live and Not Die

Legacy of Faith

Putting Your Angels to Work

The Ministry for Everyone

Let Not Your Heart Be Troubled

Worship

Faith Has No Feelings

Faith to Obtain Your Inheritance

Misguided Faith

The Master Teacher

The True Riches

The Master Teacher

Why You Should Speak in Tongues

Available at <u>www.harrisonhouse.com</u> or at any fine bookstore

The Harrison House Vision

Proclaiming the truth and the power

Of the Gospel of Jesus Christ

With excellence;

Challenging Christians to

Live victoriously,

Grow spiritually,

Know God intimately.